MONTH *by* MONTH
SCRAPBOOKING
by Amanda Probst

Creating Keepsakes
P.O. Box 420235
Palm Coast, FL 32142-0235

Toll-Free number: 888/247-5282
International: 386/597-4387

creating

creating Keepsakes

FOUNDING EDITOR Lisa Bearnson

EDITOR-IN-CHIEF Brian Tippetts

CREATIVE EDITOR Britney Mellen

SENIOR EDITOR Vanessa Hoy

SENIOR WRITER Rachel Thomae

COPY EDITOR Kim Sandoval

PROJECT COORDINATOR Liesl Russell

EDITORIAL ASSISTANTS Fred Brewer, Joannie McBride

ART DIRECTOR, SPECIAL PROJECTS Erin Bayless

SENIOR DESIGNER, SPECIAL PROJECTS Natalie Reich

PHOTOGRAPHY American Color

SENIOR PRODUCT MANAGER Dana Wilson

CK MEDIA

CHIEF EXECUTIVE OFFICER David O'Neil

CHIEF MARKETING OFFICER Andrew Johnson

CONTROLLER Scott Fambrough

VP/EDITORIAL DIRECTOR Lin Sorenson

VP/CONSUMER MARKETING Susan DuBois

VP/DIRECTOR OF EVENTS Paula Kraemer

VP/GROUP PUBLISHER Tina Battock

VP/ONLINE DIRECTOR David Harwood

SUBSCRIPTIONS
To subscribe to *Creating Keepsakes* magazine or to change the address of your current subscription, call or write:

Consumer Services
Creating Keepsakes
P.O. Box 420235
Palm Coast, FL 32142-0235

Phone: 888/247-5282
International: 386/597-4387

REPRINT PERMISSION
For information on obtaining reprints and excerpts, please contact Wrights Reprints at 877/652-5293. (Customers outside the U.S. and Canada should call 281/419-5725.)

NOTICE OF LIABILITY
The information in this book is distributed on an "as is" basis, without warranty. While every precaution has been taken in the preparation of this book, neither the author nor CK Media shall have any liability to any person or entity with respect to any liability, loss or damage caused or alleged to be caused directly or indirectly by the instructions contained in this book.

TRADEMARKS
Trademarked names are used throughout this book. Rather than put a trademark symbol in every occurrence of a trademarked name, we state we are using the names only in an editorial fashion and to the benefit of the trademark owner with no intention of infringement of the trademark.

CORPORATE OFFICES
Creating Keepsakes is located at 14850 Pony Express Road, Bluffdale, UT 84065. Phone: 801/816-8300. Fax: 801/816-8301. Home page: *www.creatingkeepsakes.com.*

Printed and bound in China.
ISBN 1-933516-85-2

www.creatingkeepsakes.com

SUMMER FULLERTON

Summer Fullerton lives in Tigard, Oregon, where she's a stay-at-home mother with two fantastic kids and a husband of 14 years. She has been scrapbooking for close to 10 years. Her favorite time of year to scrapbook is fall; she loves taking photos in September when the leaves are just beginning to turn and the sun hangs at just the right point in the sky. Summer loves her October layout and had been itching to share this particular idea for a long time. She was excited about incorporating fabric and sewing into the layout, which ties in with the "handmade" feel of the design. Summer takes January off from taking photos; she's usually still coming down from her holiday high, and it takes about half the month to recover!

LAURA KURZ

Laura Kurz lives in Baltimore, Maryland, with her husband, Ken, and their golden retriever, Charmer. Her birthday is May 22, and she constantly finds herself looking at the clock at 5:22. Laura loves the end of September, when the new television season starts. Her mom laughed when she showed her "83" layout to her; she says that having a child like Laura was difficult for a "creatively challenged" mom. Apparently, Laura was notorious for asking about Halloween costumes as early as the Fourth of July (or even earlier!).

TRACEY ODACHOWSKI

Tracey Odachowski has been scrapbooking for nearly nine years. She loves summer because her birthday is in July, and she grew up only 15 miles from the Atlantic Ocean—a great place to celebrate birthdays. She only likes winter when it's snowing in blizzard proportions because she can make her signature snow cream. September will always be a month close to her heart because that's when both of her children were born. Tracey currently resides in Newport News, Virginia, with her husband of 10 years, Chris; her son, Gabe; her daughter, Emily; and her Cavalier King Charles spaniel, Zuzu.

TIFFANY TILLMAN

Tiffany Tillman lives on the shore of Virginia with her husband and diva-daughter. While spring is her second favorite time of year, she's not too fond of April's mix of showers and allergens. September is her month of choice because she loves fall foliage. Her October layout tickles her; she's finally admitted that she, too, can be scared of nothing at all.

I peer over at the tidy, colorful stack of papers on Amanda's lap and I can't help but wonder what they are for. I've just met Amanda Probst for the first time in person (after countless e-mails and phone conversations), but I already know she's at the top of my "The Most Organized People I Know" list.

As we drive from the airport to the *Creating Keepsakes* offices, she describes the system she uses to help her turn her memories and ideas into gorgeously designed scrapbook pages. As she speaks, she slides a neatly organized binder from the stack on her lap and explains that *this* is where her ideas come to life, and while I secretly wish I was even half as organized as Amanda, I wish even *more* that I could spend an hour or two with that binder and borrow some of her ideas!

That's why I'm ecstatic over this book—a beautiful, spiral-bound selection of Amanda's fantastically creative and well-organized ideas for scrapbooking every month of the year. *Month-by-Month Scrapbooking* is a book I'll use every week and every month for many years to come and I know you will too.

Britney

Britney Mellen
Creative Editor

TRAVEL TOTE by Summer Fullerton. **Supplies** Canvas tote, fabric (for handle backing) and clear vinyl: Jo-Ann Stores; Cardstock and patterned paper: Arctic Frog; Printable iron-on transfer sheets: Hewlett-Packard; Digital brushes: Jason Gaylor, downloaded from the Internet; Composition notebook: Mead; Ribbon: American Crafts, Fancy Pants Designs and KI Memories; Travel tags and metal clip: Making Memories; Travel checklist accent: We R Memory Keepers.

SEPTEMBER

SEPTEMBER by Tracey Odachowski. **Supplies** Cardstock: Prism Papers; Patterned paper: Sassafras Lass; Punch: EK Success; Stamp: Hero Arts; Ink and pen: Stampin' Up!; Watercolor pencils: Staedtler; Fonts: ABC D'Nealian Manuscript Arrow Lines ("September") and ABC D'Nealian Manuscript (year and holidays), www.fonts4teachers.com.

GOING BACK by Amanda Probst. **Supplies** Patterned paper: Scenic Route; Letter stickers: American Crafts; Chipboard coaster: SEI; Clip and brad: Making Memories; Pen: Precision Pen, American Crafts; Font: Century Gothic, Microsoft; Other: Ribbon.

I LOVE BOOKS by Amanda Probst. **Supplies** Cardstock: Prism Papers; Chipboard brackets: BasicGrey; Paint: Making Memories; Foam letters: American Crafts; Chipboard heart: Heidi Swapp for Advantus; Font: Rockwell, Microsoft; Other: Paper clips.

FIELD TRIP by Amanda Probst. **Supplies** Cardstock: Prism Papers; Letter stickers: American Crafts; Pen: Zig Writer, EK Success.

BACK {2} SCHOOL by Summer Fullerton. **Supplies** Cardstock: Bazzill Basics Paper; Patterned paper: Doodlebug Design, KI Memories, Making Memories and Scenic Route; Decorative paper frills: Doodlebug Design; Chipboard accents: Imagination Project (date stamp) and KI Memories ("School A+"); Letter stickers: American Crafts (pink and black) and Heidi Swapp for Advantus (red); Stickers: Making Memories; Paper clip: K&Company; Label tape: Dymo.

THE ROAD AHEAD by Amanda Probst. **Supplies** Cardstock: Prism Papers; Patterned paper: 7gypsies; Felt letters: American Crafts; Font: Century Schoolbook, Microsoft.

LOVE TO READ by Laura Kurz. **Supplies** Patterned paper: Scenic Route; Journaling block: Heidi Swapp for Advantus; Chipboard letter: Li'l Davis Designs; Metal tab: Making Memories; Font: Splendid 66, Internet.

ART CLASS by Amanda Probst. **Supplies** Cardstock: Prism Papers; Felt letters: American Crafts; Sealer: Mod Podge, Plaid Enterprises; Ink: Adirondack Alcohol Inks, Ranger Industries; Font: Century Schoolbook, Microsoft. Idea to note: To create the inked background, Amanda first applied Mod Podge to the cardstock to prevent the alcohol ink from soaking in. When dry, she applied the alcohol ink with a roller and dripped a few spots of the blue ink. To finish, she added a few drops of rubbing alcohol to create a watery effect.

JUST ONE GLANCE by Tiffany Tillman. **Supplies** Software: Adobe Photoshop CS3, Adobe Systems; Cardstock: Prism Papers; Patterned paper: American Crafts; Font: Georgia, Microsoft.

THINGS I WANT TO LEARN by Amanda Probst. **Supplies** Cardstock: Prism Papers; Cookie sheet: Target; Shrinkable plastic: Shrinky Dinks, K & B Innovations, Inc.; Magnets: Pro MAG; Eyelets: We R Memory Keepers; Ribbon: BasicGrey; Gaffer tape: 7gypsies; Fonts: CK Little Al, www.scrapnfonts.com; Century Gothic, Microsoft; Kids, www.scrapvillage.com.

OCTOBER

OCTOBER by Amanda Probst. **Supplies** Cardstock: Prism Papers; Flashcards (title): 7gypsies; Stamps: 7gypsies (square) and Hero Arts (leaf and tree); Ink: ColorBox, Clearsnap; Pen: Precision Pen, American Crafts.

SETTING THE STAGE by Amanda Probst. **Supplies** Cardstock: Prism Papers; Patterned paper: Creative Imaginations; Chipboard letters: American Crafts; Letter stickers: EK Success; Buttons: foof-a-La, Autumn Leaves; Ribbon: Heidi Swapp for Advantus and May Arts; Pens: Precision Pen (black), American Crafts, Artist (orange), Marvy Uchida; Uni-ball Signo (white), Sanford; Fonts: Century Gothic (journaling), Microsoft; LD Painter's Hand, www.scrapnfonts.com.

COSTUMES by Amanda Probst. **Supplies** Cardstock: Prism Papers; Letter stickers: Around the Block; Chipboard coaster: Imagination Project; Font: CK Jessica, www.scrapnfonts.com.

EWW . . . by Amanda Probst. **Supplies** Cardstock: Prism Papers; Chipboard letters: Li'l Davis Designs; Felt flower border: Queen & Co.; Font: Tahoma, Microsoft.

83 by Laura Kurz. **Supplies** Cardstock: American Crafts; Patterned paper: Scenic Route; Chipboard letters: Heidi Swapp for Advantus; Rub-on and pin: Heidi Grace Designs; Font: Times New Roman, Microsoft.

GLOW by Amanda Probst. **Supplies** Cardstock: Prism Papers; Shimmer stickers: Making Memories; Pen: Precision Pen, American Crafts.

EARTH'S ALIENS by Tiffany Tillman. **Supplies** Software: Adobe Photoshop CS3, Adobe Systems; Cardstock: Prism Papers; Patterned paper: Brads: Making Memories; Chipboard heart: Heidi Swapp for Advantus; Chipboard sign: KI Memories; Letters: Queen & Co.; Fonts: Alienator, www.dafont.com; Impact and Bank Gothic, Internet.

LEAF ATTACK by Amanda Probst. **Supplies** Cardstock: Prism Papers; Patterned paper, arrow and metal tab: 7gypsies; Bookplate and brads: BasicGrey; Chipboard letters: BasicGrey, Fancy Pants Designs, Heidi Swapp for Advantus ("leaf") and Rusty Pickle; Paint: Making Memories; Pen: Precision Pen, American Crafts.

HANDMADE HALLOWEEN by Summer Fullerton. **Supplies** Cardstock: Bazzill Basics Paper; Patterned paper: BasicGrey; Jewels and chipboard letters: Heidi Swapp for Advantus; Paint: Plaid Enterprises; Felt stickers and acrylic heart: American Crafts; Stick pin: Boxer Scrapbook Productions; Tag: Making Memories; Font: Century Gothic, Microsoft.

MINI WREATH/CANDLE BASE by Tracey Odachowski. **Supplies** Cardstock: Stampin' Up!; Watercolor pencils: Staedtler; Wreath, berries and acorns: Michaels; Digital cutter: Xyron Wishblade; Other: Hot glue.

NOVEMBER

NOVEMBER by Tiffany Tillman. **Supplies** Cardstock: Prism Papers; Patterned paper: BasicGrey, Dream Street Papers and KI Memories; Rub-ons: Melissa Frances; Stickers: Urban Lily; Pen: Bic.

BOUNTIFUL by Amanda Probst. **Supplies** Cardstock: Prism Papers; Fabric paper: Love, Elsie for KI Memories; Letter stickers: Li'l Davis Designs; Font: Rockwell, Microsoft.

4TH THURSDAY OF NOVEMBEr by Amanda Probst. **Supplies** Cardstock: Prism Papers; Mailing labels: Paper Source; Recipe card: My Mind's Eye; Letter stickers: American Crafts; Stamp: Hero Arts; Ink: ColorBox, Clearsnap; Font: Century Gothic, Microsoft.

OY by Amanda Probst. **Supplies** Cardstock: Prism Papers; Patterned paper: BasicGrey (strips cut from the sample page that comes with the collection); Chipboard letters: Rusty Pickle; Paint: Making Memories; Stamp: FontWerks; Ink: ColorBox, Clearsnap; Pen: Precision Pen, American Crafts; Font: Palatino, Microsoft.

GIVE THANKS by Summer Fullerton. **Supplies** Cardstock: Prism Papers; Patterned paper and decorative stickers: KI Memories; Chipboard letters: Chatterbox; Letter stickers: American Crafts; Decorative-edge scissors: Fiskars; Font: Century Gothic, Microsoft.

COMMUNITY SERVICE by Amanda Probst. **Supplies** Cardstock: Prism Papers; Patterned paper and letter stickers: American Crafts; Epoxy stickers: Love, Elsie for KI Memories; Font: Century Gothic, Microsoft.

I DON'T VOTE by Tracey Odachowski. **Supplies** Cardstock: Bazzill Basics Paper, Club Scrap and Wausau Paper; Rub-ons: I lambly Studios; Digital cutter: Xyron Wishblade; Font: Arial, Microsoft.

THANK FULL by Amanda Probst. **Supplies** Cardstock: Prism Papers; Transparency: Hammermill; Paint: Adirondack Paint Dabbers, Ranger Industries; Brads: Creative Impressions; Fonts: LD Painter's Hand ("Thank"), downloaded from www.scrapnfonts.com; Impact ("Full") and Rockwell (journaling), Microsoft; Other: Hinge.

UNCONDITIONAL LOVE by Laura Kurz. **Supplies** Patterned paper: Tinkering Ink; Letter sticker: Martha Stewart Crafts; Font: Century Gothic, Microsoft.

"GRATITUDE" JOURNAL by Amanda Probst. **Supplies** Chipboard album: Maya Road; Cardstock: Prism Papers; Stamp: Hero Arts; Ink: ColorBox, Clearsnap; Embossing powder: Stamp World; Felt flowers: American Crafts; Decorative brad: Making Memories; Pen: Precision Pen, American Crafts; Other: Feathers.

DECEMBER

DECEMBER by Amanda Probst. **Supplies** Cardstock: Prism Papers; Ribbon: American Crafts, BasicGrey, Bobbin Ribbon, Making Memories and May Arts; Rub-on numbers: Making Memories; Stamps: Hero Arts; Ink: ColorBox, Clearsnap; Epoxy stickers: KI Memories; Pen: Precision Pen, American Crafts.

THE PHOTO by Amanda Probst. **Supplies** Cardstock: Prism Papers; Patterned paper: Imaginisce; Bookplate: BasicGrey; Jeweled brads: Magic Scraps; Fabric tag: Karen Foster Design; Pen: Precision Pen, American Crafts; Fonts: Impact (title) and Eras (journaling), Microsoft.

PRESENT by Amanda Probst. **Supplies** Cardstock: Prism Papers; Patterned paper: BasicGrey and KI Memories; Letter tiles: Provo Craft; Clear page pebbles: Creative Imaginations; Pen: Precision Pen, American Crafts; Font: Century Gothic, Microsoft; Other: Transparency images (taken from an old Christmas card).

YAY 4 SNOW by Amanda Probst. **Supplies** Patterned paper: BasicGrey; Letter stickers: Making Memories; Foam letters: American Crafts; Number flashcard: 7gypsies; Acrylic snowflakes: Doodlebug Design and Heidi Grace Designs; Snowflake brad: Treasured Memories; Jeweled brad: Better Office; Pen: Zig Writer, EK Success; Font: CK Chemistry, www.scrapnfonts.com; Other: Felt snowflakes and jewel.

PRESENT EXCHANGE by Tiffany Tillman. **Supplies** Software: Adobe Photoshop CS3, Adobe Systems; Digital patterned paper: Cuddlebug by Shabby Princess, www.theshabbyshoppe.com; Digital ribbon: Be Yourself Page Set by Kim Christensen, www.scrapartist.com; Digital title label: Anticipation by Leora Sanford, www.littledreamerdesigns.com; Digital staples: Katie Pertiet, www.designerdigitals.com.

WORTH REMEMBERING by Amanda Probst. **Supplies** Cardstock: Prism Papers; Stamp: Marcella by Kay; Ink: ColorBox, Clearsnap; Fonts: Century Gothic and Rockwell, Microsoft; Other: Stamps from Amanda's collection.

YOUR STORY by Summer Fullerton. **Supplies** Cardstock: Bazzill Basics Paper; Patterned paper: A2Z Essentials, Around the Block, FontWerks, Making Memories and My Mind's Eye; Chipboard shapes: American Crafts; Brads: Queen & Co. and SEI; Tag: Making Memories; Rub-ons: BasicGrey and Hambly Studios; Stamp: Hero Arts; Ink: ColorBox, Clearsnap; Sticker: Creative Imaginations; Other: Staples.

GIRLS WOULDN'T DO THAT by Amanda Probst. **Supplies** Cardstock: Prism Papers; Patterned paper, foam letters and ribbon: American Crafts; Letter stickers: Heidi Swapp for Advantus; Font: Century Gothic, Microsoft.

OUR WONDERFUL LIFE by Tracey Odachowski. **Supplies** Cardstock: Bazzill Basics Paper; Patterned paper and letter stickers: BasicGrey; Stamps: Stampin' Up!; Ink: Ink It Up (silver and gold) and Stampin' Up! (red, green and brown); Watercolor pencils: Staedtler; Gold pen: Sharpie, Sanford; Font: Santa's Sleigh, Internet.

TAKE NOTE by Laura Kurz. **Supplies** Album: Close To My Heart; Cardstock: Prism Papers; Patterned paper: Tinkering Ink; Stamps: FontWerks and Paper Source; Ink: Top Boss Tinted Embossing Ink, Clearsnap; Rub-ons: American Crafts; Pin: Heidi Grace Designs.

{ CONTENTS }

PHOTO TAG *by Amanda Probst.* **Supplies** *Cardstock:* Prism Papers; *Letter stickers:* American Crafts; *Chipboard letters:* We R Memory Keepers; *Paint:* Making Memories; *Gaffer tape:* 7gypsies; *Brads:* Paper Studio; *Label tape:* Dymo; *Pen:* Precision Pen, American Crafts; *Font:* Rockwell, Microsoft.

SIGNS OF SPRING *by Tiffany Tillman.* **Supplies** *Software:* Adobe Photoshop CS3, Adobe Systems; *Digital patterned paper:* Grace by Katie Pertiet, Anticipation by Leora Sanford, Pink Sonata by Mindy Terasawa, all from *www.designerdigitals.com;* Olivia Collection by Shabby Princess, *www.theshabbyshoppe.com; Digital Sanford staples:* Flat Jack by Katie Pertiet, *www.designerdigitals.com; stickers:* In My Garden by Leora Sanford, *www.designerdigitals.com; Digital frames:* Dirty by Katie Pertiet, *www.designerdigitals.com; Digital title paper:* I Dream in Paisley by Heather Melzer, *www.heatheranndesigns.com; Digital paper tears:* Torn and Curled Paper Edges #2 by Jen Caputo, *www.scrapbookgraphics.com; Font:* 28 Days Later, Teletype.

GARDEN JOURNAL *by Laura Kurz.* **Supplies** *Album:* We R Memory Keepers; *Patterned paper:* Sassafras Lass and Scenic Route; *Foliage stamp:* FontWerks; *Ink:* Top Boss Tinted Embossing Ink, Clearsnap; *Letter stickers:* Heidi Swapp for Advantus; *Paint:* Making Memories; *Font:* Print Clearly, Internet.

MAY

MAY *by Amanda Probst.* **Supplies** *Cardstock:* Prism Papers; *Patterned paper:* American Crafts, Basic Grey, Collage Press, Fancy Pants Designs, KI Memories and Making Memories; *Foam letters:* American Crafts; *Stamps:* Autumn Leaves (days) and Hero Arts (bee); *Ink:* ColorBox, Clearsnap; VersaMark, Tsukineko; *Embossing powder:* All Night Media; *Pens:* Precision Pen, American Crafts; Uni-ball Signo (white), Sanford; *Other:* Felt flowers.

MEMORIAL DAYS *by Amanda Probst. Photos by Cassandra Smith.* **Supplies** *Cardstock:* Prism Papers; *Vellum:* The Paper Company; *Photo corners:* Heidi Swapp for Advantus; *Fonts:* Charlemagne (title) and Palatino (journaling), Microsoft.

ALWAYS MOM *by Amanda Probst.* **Supplies** *Cardstock:* Prism Papers; *Patterned paper, letter stickers and pen:* American Crafts; *Chipboard coaster:* SEI; *Chipboard photo corner:* Imagination Project; *Other:* Jewels.

CHALK-O-RIF-FIC *by Amanda Probst.* **Supplies** *Cardstock:* Prism Papers; *Patterned paper:* BasicGrey (pink), KI Memories (yellow) and My Mind's Eye (blue, green); *Felt photo corners:* American Crafts; *Pens:* Precision Pen (black), American Crafts; Artist (orange), Marvy Uchida; *Pastel pencils:* Gioconda, Koh-I-Noor; *Fonts:* Alba Super (title) and Eras Demi (journaling), Microsoft.

CROP GALS *by Tracey Odachowski.* **Supplies** *Cardstock:* Stampin' Up!; *Patterned paper:* Scenic Route; *Metallic paper and transparency frame:* Hambly Studios; *Chipboard letters and jewels:* Heidi Swapp for Advantus; *Flowers:* Prima; *Ribbon:* BasicGrey; *Font:* University Roman LET, *www.searchfreefonts.com.*

FOR ME? *by Amanda Probst.* **Supplies** *Cardstock:* Prism Papers; *Patterned paper:* BasicGrey; *Felt letters:* American Crafts; *Flower die cut:* Deluxe Cuts; *Font:* Typist, *www.scrapvillage.com.*

DON'T TELL MY BOSS *by Laura Kurz.* **Supplies** *Patterned paper:* Creative Imaginations; *Rub-ons:* Heidi Grace Designs; *Font:* Splendid 66, Internet; *Other:* Photo corners.

MY DAD'S MOM *by Amanda Probst.* **Supplies** *Cardstock:* Prism Papers; *Patterned paper and foam letters:* American Crafts; *Font:* Palatino, Microsoft.

FROM THE HEART *by Summer Fullerton.* **Supplies** *Cardstock:* Bazzill Basics Paper and Prism Papers; *Patterned paper:* Arctic Frog, BasicGrey and Making Memories; *Chipboard letters:* We R Memory Keepers; *Chipboard shape:* BasicGrey; *Stamps:* Hero Arts; *Ink:* ColorBox, Clearsnap; Ranger Industries; *Paint:* Plaid Enterprises; *Flower and tag:* Making Memories; *Font:* Avant Garde, Internet.

"FAMILIA" MATCHING GAME *by Tiffany Tillman.* **Supplies** *Chipboard box and pieces:* Maya Road; *Patterned paper:* Cloud 9 Design; *Chipboard:* Family Collection, Spanish Memories Inc.

JUNE

JUNE *by Laura Kurz.* **Supplies** *Cardstock:* Tinkering Ink; *Patterned paper:* American Crafts; *Rub-ons:* Heidi Grace Designs; *Letter stickers:* Heidi Swapp for Advantus; *Font:* Splendid 66, Internet.

CHERRY HARVEST *by Amanda Probst.* **Supplies** *Cardstock:* Prism Papers; *Patterned paper:* Love, Elsie for KI Memories; *Ribbon:* BasicGrey; *Chipboard coaster:* Imagination Project; *Rub-on letters and graphic:* American Crafts; *Corner-rounder punch:* EK Success; *Pens:* Precision Pen, American Crafts; Artist, Marvy Uchida; *Font:* Century Schoolbook, Microsoft.

JUST ADD WATER *by Amanda Probst.* **Supplies** *Cardstock:* Prism Papers; *Acetate letters and ribbon:* Heidi Swapp for Advantus; *Ink:* Adirondack Alcohol Inks, Ranger Industries; *Ribbon buckle:* Bazzill Basics Paper; *Letter stickers:* American Crafts; *Font:* Tahoma, Microsoft.

FATHERS & SONS *by Amanda Probst.* **Supplies** *Cardstock:* Prism Papers; *Letter stickers:* Making Memories; *Brads:* Paper Studio; *Font:* Palatino, Microsoft; *Other:* Tag and jewel.

A TASTE OF SUMMER *by Tiffany Tillman.* **Supplies** *Software:* Adobe Photoshop CS3, Adobe Systems; *Patterned paper and chipboard:* Scenic Route; *Font:* Georgia, Microsoft.

PAUSE *by Amanda Probst.* **Supplies** *Cardstock:* Prism Papers; *Chipboard letters:* Pressed Petals; *Rub-on:* My Mind's Eye; *Pen:* Zig Writer, EK Success; *Font:* Rockwell, Microsoft.

SUMMER IS . . . *by Summer Fullerton.* **Supplies** *Cardstock:* Bazzill Basics Paper and Prism Papers; *Patterned paper:* Making Memories; *Chipboard letters and shape:* Li'l Davis Designs; *Stamp:* Hero Arts; *Glue, glitter and paint:* Plaid Enterprises; *Felt brackets:* American Crafts; *Buttons:* foof-a-La, Autumn Leaves; *Brads:* Queen & Co.; *Font:* Prissy Frat Boy, Internet.

WHAT DADDY DOES *by Amanda Probst.* **Supplies** *Cardstock:* Prism Papers; *Patterned paper:* BasicGrey; *Transparency:* Hambly Studios; *Photo corners:* Pioneer; *Font:* Rockwell, Microsoft.

MY FAVORITE SUMMER FOODS *by Tracey Odachowski.* **Supplies** *Cardstock:* Bazzill Basics Paper; *Patterned paper and letter stickers:* Dream Street Papers; *Rub-ons:* American Crafts (heart) and Chatterbox (letters); *Scalloped die cuts:* Doodlebug Design; *Pens:* Sharpie (white), Sanford; Stampin' Up! (pink and blue).

"WHAT 2 DO" JAR *by Amanda Probst.* **Supplies** *Glass jar:* Anchor Hocking; *Ink:* Adirondack Alcohol Inks, Ranger Industries; *Patterned paper:* Collage Press; *Cardstock:* Prism Papers; *Ribbon and letter stickers:* American Crafts; *Brad:* Creative Impressions; *Washer:* Making Memories; *Font:* Century Gothic, Microsoft; *Other:* Spinner.

JULY

JULY *by Summer Fullerton.* **Supplies** *Cardstock:* Bazzill Basics Paper; *Patterned paper:* A2Z Essentials, American Crafts, Bo-Bunny Press, Creative Imaginations, FontWerks and Scenic Route; *Stamp:* 7gypsies; *Stickers:* Imagination Project; *Letter stickers and chipboard shape:* American Crafts; *4th of July accent:* Doodlebug Design; *Rub-ons:* Heidi Grace Designs; *Punch:* Fiskars; *Font:* Avant Garde, Internet.

MONTANA IN JULY *by Amanda Probst.* **Supplies** *Cardstock:* Prism Papers; *Letter stickers:* American Crafts and Creative Imaginations; *Ribbon:* Heidi Swapp for Advantus; *Chipboard stars:* Li'l Davis Designs; *Flowers:* Bazzill Basics Paper and Li'l Davis Designs; *Font:* Century Schoolbook, Microsoft.

FIREWORKS *by Amanda Probst.* **Supplies** *Cardstock:* Prism Papers; *Letter stickers:* American Crafts; *Fireworks embellishments:* Jolee's by EK Success; *Font:* Rockwell, Microsoft.

BLISS *by Amanda Probst.* **Supplies** *Cardstock:* Prism Papers; *Acetate letters:* Heidi Swapp for Advantus; *Ink:* Adirondack Alcohol Inks, Ranger Industries; *Letter stickers:* Making Memories; *Stamp:* Hero Arts; *Ink:* VersaMark, Tsukineko; *Other:* Transparency.

WHAT HAPPENED? *by Laura Kurz.* **Supplies** *Cardstock:* Bazzill Basics Paper; *Chipboard stars:* Li'l Davis Designs; *Rub-on letters:* American Crafts; *Letter stickers:* Heidi Swapp for Advantus; *Font:* Century Gothic, Microsoft.

SUMMER READING *by Amanda Probst.* **Supplies** *Cardstock:* Prism Papers; *Metal tab:* Making Memories; *Fonts:* Impact and Rockwell, Microsoft; *Other:* Amanda created the patterned paper by scanning illustrations from *Akiko on the Planet Smoo* by Mark Crilley.

I'M PROUD OF YOU *by Tracey Odachowski.* **Supplies** *Cardstock:* Wausau Paper; *Patterned paper:* Cosmo Cricket (light green) and Daisy D's Paper Co. (red and blue); *Rub-ons:* Daisy D's Paper Co.; *Foam stickers:* American Crafts; *Fabric stars:* Making Memories; *Pens:* American Crafts (white) and Stampin' Up! (black); *Watercolor pencils:* Staedtler; *Digital cutter:* Xyron, Wishblade; *Font:* Baskerville Old Face, Microsoft; *Other:* Vellum.

B-17 *by Amanda Probst.* **Supplies** *Cardstock:* Prism Papers; *Chipboard shape:* Li'l Davis Designs; *Fonts:* Rockwell, Microsoft; PussyCat, Internet.

HISTORIC PHOTOS *by Tiffany Tillman.* **Supplies** *Software:* Adobe Photoshop CS3, Adobe Systems; *Cardstock:* Prism Papers; *Patterned paper:* BasicGrey and Imaginisce; *Circle punch:* EK Success; *Flowers:* Making Memories; *Letter stickers:* Arctic Frog; *Chipboard:* Out of Town Chipboard Circles, Scenic Route; *Font:* Teletype, Internet.

"NOW" CLOCK *by Amanda Probst.* **Supplies** *Clock kit:* Across the Street; *Patterned paper:* Tinkering Ink; *Dimensional glaze:* Glossy Accents, Ranger Industries; *Clock hands:* Walnut Hollow; *Chipboard letters:* Heidi Swapp for Advantus; *Fonts:* CK Fast Food, *www.scrapnfonts.com;* Rockwell, Microsoft.

AUGUST

AUGUST *by Amanda Probst.* **Supplies** *Cardstock:* Prism Papers; *Number masks:* Heidi Swapp for Advantus; *Letter and number stickers:* Li'l Davis Designs (also used as masks); *Paint:* Adirondack Paint Dabbers, Ranger Industries; *License-plate stickers:* Sticker Studio; *Pen:* Precision Pen, American Crafts.

IN THE CAR *by Amanda Probst.* **Supplies** *Cardstock:* Prism Papers; *Patterned paper:* K&Company; *Chipboard letters:* Chatterbox; *Ribbon:* BasicGrey and May Arts; *License plate:* Karen Foster Design; *Transparency:* Making Memories; *Font:* Century Schoolbook, Microsoft.

OUR LIST *by Amanda Probst.* **Supplies** *Cardstock:* Prism Papers; *Patterned paper:* KI Memories; *Stamps:* FontWerks; *Ink:* ColorBox, Clearsnap; *Pastel pencil:* Gioconda, Koh-I-Noor; *Pens:* Precision Pen, American Crafts; Artist, Marvy Uchida; Gelly Roll Glaze, Sakura; *Fonts:* Century Gothic, Microsoft; CK Chemistry, CK Fast Food, CK Evie, CK Jessica, CK Surfer, CK Leisurely, CK Tatty and LD Painter's Hand, *www.scrapnfonts.com;* Renaissance, *www.twopeasinabucket.com;* Santa's Sleigh and Pegsanna, *www.scrapvillage.com;* Rockwell, Microsoft.

REINTRODUCTION *by Amanda Probst.* **Supplies** *Cardstock:* Prism Papers; *Patterned paper:* Chatterbox, KI Memories and Scenic Route; *Acetate letters, flower and metal slides:* Heidi Swapp for Advantus; *Letter stickers:* American Crafts; *Ribbon:* BasicGrey; *Bookcloth words:* Chatterbox; *Definition sticker and brad:* Making Memories; *Chipboard button:* KI Memories; *Font:* Rockwell, Microsoft; *Other:* Sheer leaf.

HERSHEY *by Tracey Odachowski.* **Supplies** *Cardstock:* Wausau Paper; *Patterned and solid paper:* American Crafts; *Letter stickers:* Making Memories; *Label sticker:* 7gypsies; *Pen:* Stampin' Up!.

HOMETOWN ADVENTURE *by Amanda Probst.* **Supplies** *Cardstock:* Prism Papers; *Patterned paper:* My Mind's Eye; *Foam letters:* American Crafts; *Chipboard shapes:* Scenic Route; *Font:* Tahoma, Microsoft.

SPOT *by Tiffany Tillman.* **Supplies** *Software:* Adobe Photoshop CS3, Adobe Systems; *Digital patterned paper and elements:* Surf's Up Kit by Mindy Terasawa, *www.designerdigitals.com; Digital title stamps:* Grimey Alphabet by Katie Pertiet, *www.designerdigitals.com; Digital paper tears:* Torn and Curled Paper Edges #2 by Jen Caputo, *www.scrapbookgraphics.com.*

SHADOW PLAY *by Amanda Probst.* **Supplies** *Cardstock:* Prism Papers; *Pencil:* Sanford; *Fonts:* Elephant (title) and Tahoma (journaling), Microsoft.

SCOTLAND *by Laura Kurz.* **Supplies** *Patterned paper:* American Crafts and My Mind's Eye; *Chipboard letters:* Li'l Davis Designs; *Metal tab and travel sticker:* Making Memories; *Star tape:* Heidi Swapp for Advantus.

{ AMANDA'S NOTE }

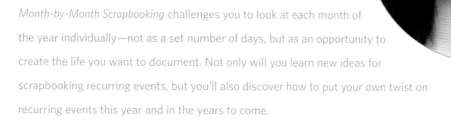

Raise your hand if you almost dread taking Christmas morning pictures, knowing you'll have to come up with something—*anything*—to say about them in your scrapbook. Raise your hand if you have piles of old Halloween pictures you just can't seem to get caught up on . . . or if you'd really like to scrapbook your own childhood but don't have a clue where to start. Guess what—this book is for you!

Month-by-Month Scrapbooking challenges you to look at each month of the year individually—not as a set number of days, but as an opportunity to create the life you want to document. Not only will you learn new ideas for scrapbooking recurring events, but you'll also discover how to put your own twist on recurring events this year and in the years to come.

The book is broken into chapters by month. Within each chapter, you'll find layouts that focus on the different aspects of scrapbooking: journaling, design, concept and photography. You'll also find a calendar page and a project for each month.

My contributors and I have had so much fun creating this book for you. I hope you'll enjoy your journey through the year with us!

Amanda

Amanda Probst
Contributing Editor

{ SUPPLIES }

JANUARY

JANUARY *by Amanda Probst.* **Supplies** *Cardstock:* Prism Papers; *Embossed paper:* Doodlebug Design; *Pens:* Precision Pen, American Crafts; VersaMarker, Tsukineko; *Rub-on graphic:* Dee's Designs; *Fonts:* Impact, Microsoft; CK Fast Food, www.scrapnfonts.com; *Other:* Jewels.

EVE & DAY *by Amanda Probst.* **Supplies** *Cardstock:* Prism Papers; *Patterned paper:* Luxe Designs; *Chipboard letters:* American Crafts; *Chipboard sign:* BasicGrey; *Paint:* Making Memories; *Font:* CK Chemistry, www.scrapnfonts.com.

NOTE TO SELF *by Amanda Probst.* **Supplies** *Cardstock:* Prism Papers; *Patterned paper:* K&Company and Amy Butler Design; "Note to Self" paper: Knock, Knock; *Monograms:* My Mind's Eye (used to make background); *Chalk pencils:* Gioconda, Koh-I-Noor; *Pen:* Precision Pen, American Crafts; *Font:* Rockwell, Microsoft.

SNOWBALL MAKER *by Amanda Probst.* **Supplies** *Cardstock:* Prism Papers; *Patterned paper:* SEI; *Foam letters:* American Crafts; *Photo corners:* Pioneer; *Pen:* Precision Pen, American Crafts; *Font:* Century Old Style, Microsoft; *Other:* Jewels.

MIDNIGHT KISSES *by Tracey Odachowski.* **Supplies** *Cardstock:* Bazzill Basics Paper; *Patterned paper, letter stickers and die cuts:* BasicGrey; *Clock hands:* Tracey's own design; *Ink:* VersaMark, Tsukineko; *Digital cutter:* Xyron; *Wishblade font:* Century Gothic, Microsoft; *Other:* Brad.

SPECIAL NIGHTS *by Amanda Probst.* **Supplies** *Cardstock:* Prism Papers; *Patterned paper:* Scenic Route; *Chipboard letters and border:* Li'l Davis Designs; *Font:* Century Gothic, Microsoft.

WE WILL *by Laura Kurz.* **Supplies** *Patterned paper:* Daisy D's Paper Co.; *Rub-ons:* FontWerks; *Number stickers:* Heidi Swapp for Advantus; *Font:* Print Clearly, Internet.

ME *by Amanda Probst.* **Supplies** *Cardstock:* Prism Papers; *Sheer letters:* Maya Road; *Transparency flourish:* My Mind's Eye; *Rub-on:* Hambly Studios; *Label tape:* Dymo; *Letter stickers:* Making Memories. *Idea to note:* Amanda printed the background photos on white cardstock.

BYE *by Summer Fullerton.* **Supplies** *Cardstock:* Bazzill Basics Paper and Prism Papers; *Patterned paper:* A2Z Essentials and BasicGrey; *Chipboard letters:* Heidi Swapp for Advantus; *Jewels:* Doodlebug Design; *Ribbon:* BasicGrey; *Font:* Avant Garde, Internet; *Other:* Staples.

"WHO AM I?" JOURNAL CARDS *by Tiffany Tillman.* **Supplies** *Software:* Adobe Photoshop CS3, Adobe Systems; *Digital patterned paper:* Funktastic Kraft by Two Sisters Designs, www.scrapartist.com; The Wonderful Collection by Shabby Princess, www.theshabbyshoppe.com; Carriage House by Iron Orchid Designs, www.acherryontop.com; Ledger Sun Print Paper Pack by Katie Pertiet; Surf's Up Kit and Dog Gone Cute Kit by Mindy Terasawa; Jungle Cruise Paper Pack by Kellie Mize; all from www.designerdigitals.com; A Child Is Born by Denise Docherty; *Digital accent:* Flower Flourish Brushes by Jessie Edwards, www.designerdigitals.com; *Chipboard accent:* Urban Lily; *Font:* Courier New, Internet.

FEBRUARY

FEBRUARY *by Amanda Probst.* **Supplies** *Cardstock:* Prism Papers; *Specialty paper:* Paper Source; *Title card:* Every Jot & Tittle; *Stamps:* Hero Arts; *Ink:* ColorBox, Clearsnap; VersaMark, Tsukineko; *Dimensional paint:* Ranger Industries; *Chipboard heart:* Heidi Swapp for Advantus; *Pen:* Precision Pen, American Crafts; *Other:* Ribbon.

FEBRUARYS *by Amanda Probst.* **Supplies** *Cardstock:* Prism Papers and KI Memories (lace); *Number flashcard:* 7gypsies; *Ribbon:* BasicGrey and Prima; *Label tape:* Dymo; *Brads:* Making Memories and Target; *Chipboard accent:* Heidi Swapp for Advantus; *Font:* CK Chemistry, www.scrapnfonts.com.

YOU'RE MINE *by Amanda Probst.* **Supplies** *Cardstock:* Prism Papers; *Patterned paper and chipboard buttons:* KI Memories; *Foam letters:* American Crafts; *Pens:* Precision Pen and Galaxy Marker, American Crafts; *Other:* Jewels.

THEN & THEN *by Amanda Probst.* **Supplies** *Cardstock:* Prism Papers; *Patterned paper:* BasicGrey; *Chipboard letters:* Li'l Davis Designs; *Letter stickers:* American Crafts (title) and EK Success (names); *Ribbon:* Doodlebug Design; *Gaffer tape and word strips:* 7gypsies; *Brads:* Making Memories; *Label tape:* Dymo; *Pens:* Precision Pen (black), Artist (orange), Marvy Uchida; *Font:* CK Chemistry, www.scrapnfonts.com.

ONE BOY, ONE GIRL *by Laura Kurz.* **Supplies** *Patterned paper:* Making Memories; *Transparency:* Hambly Studios; *Plastic letters:* Heidi Swapp for Advantus; *Pin:* Heidi Grace Designs; *Rub-on:* Daisy D's Paper Co.; *Font:* Print Clearly, Internet.

THE POWER OF WORDS *by Amanda Probst.* **Supplies** *Cardstock:* Prism Papers; *Patterned paper:* Fancy Pants Designs and My Mind's Eye; *Ribbon:* American Crafts and May Arts; *Fonts:* Century Schoolbook and Impact, Microsoft.

JINXY *by Tiffany Tillman.* **Supplies** *Cardstock:* Prism Papers and WorldWin; *Patterned paper:* 7gypsies; *Epoxy stickers:* Love, Elsie for KI Memories; *Font:* Courier New, Microsoft.

A LOVE AFFAIR WITH FOOD *by Amanda Probst.* **Supplies** *Cardstock:* Prism Papers; *Patterned paper:* Scenic Route; *Letter stamps:* FontWerks; *Ink:* ColorBox, Clearsnap; *Pastel pencil:* Gioconda, Koh-I-Noor; *Buttons:* foof-a-La, Autumn Leaves; *Font:* Arial Narrow, Microsoft Word. *Idea to note:* Amanda filled in the stamped letter with a white pastel pencil.

BILTMORE *by Tracey Odachowski.* **Supplies** *Cardstock:* Prism Papers; *Patterned transparencies:* Hambly Studios; *Fonts:* Saffron Too (title), www.urbanfonts.com; Dustismo Roman (journaling), www.dustismo.com.

HOW SWEET IT IS . . . *by Summer Fullerton.* **Supplies** *Cardstock:* Bazzill Basics Paper; *Patterned paper and chipboard shape:* BasicGrey; *Felt:* Jo-Ann Stores; *Stamp:* Hero Arts; *Ink:* ColorBox, Ranger Industries; *Scissors:* Fiskars; *Font:* Avant Garde, Internet.

I LOVE THEE . . . *by Summer Fullerton.* **Supplies** *Cardstock:* Prism Papers; *Patterned paper:* BasicGrey, KI Memories and Scenic Route; *Felt flower:* American Crafts; *Stamp:* Hero Arts; *Ink:* ColorBox, Clearsnap; Ranger Industries.

BE MINE *by Summer Fullerton.* **Supplies** *Cardstock:* Bazzill Basics Papers and Prism Papers; *Patterned paper:* foof-a-La, Autumn Leaves; *Tag:* Making Memories; *Brads:* Queen & Co.; *Punch:* Fiskars; *Other:* Lollipop.

MARCH

MARCH *by Amanda Probst.* **Supplies** *Cardstock:* Prism Papers; *Patterned paper:* Collage Press and Scenic Route; *Decorative brads and paint:* Making Memories; *Chipboard letters:* Fancy Pants Designs; *Stamps:* FontWerks (foliage and numbers) and Hero Arts (clover); *Ink:* ColorBox, Clearsnap; Stampin' Up!; *Pastel pencils:* Gioconda, Koh-I-Noor; *Pen:* Precision Pen, American Crafts; *Other:* Flowers.

GREEN POPCORN & PINCHING *by Amanda Probst.* **Supplies** *Cardstock:* Prism Papers; *Stamp:* FontWerks; *Ink:* ColorBox, Clearsnap; *Pastel pencil:* Gioconda, Koh-I-Noor; *Green pen:* Gelly Roll Glaze, Sakura; *Fonts:* Impact, Microsoft; CK Tatty and LD Painter's Hand, www.scrapnfonts.com; Typist, www.scrapvillage.com.

SOME THINGS NEVER CHANGE *by Amanda Probst.* **Supplies** *Cardstock:* Prism Papers; *Patterned paper:* American Crafts, KI Memories and Scenic Route; *Ribbon:* Basic Grey; *Chipboard letter circle:* Heidi Swapp for Advantus; *Rub-on graphic:* Creative Imaginations; *Pen:* Precision Pen, American Crafts; *Fonts:* Blue Plate Special, www.scrapvillage.com; Century Gothic, Microsoft.

TREASURE *by Amanda Probst.* **Supplies** *Cardstock:* Prism Papers; *Patterned paper:* Sandylion; *Stamp:* Heidi Swapp for Advantus; *Ink:* ColorBox, Clearsnap; *Fiber:* BasicGrey; *Stickers:* Creative Imaginations; *Clear pen:* Gelly Roll Glaze, Sakura; *Font:* Garamond, Microsoft.

LOVE THEM BAD EGGS *by Tiffany Tillman.* **Supplies** *Cardstock:* Prism Papers; *Patterned paper:* American Crafts and KI Memories; *Chipboard heart:* Heidi Swapp for Advantus; *Letter stickers:* Arctic Frog and KI Memories.

LIFE IS GOOD *by Amanda Probst.* **Supplies** *Cardstock:* Prism Papers; *Embossed paper:* Doodlebug Design; *Rub-on title:* Daisy D's Paper Co.; *Paint:* Making Memories; *Tulle ribbon:* Heidi Swapp for Advantus; *Pen:* Precision Pen, American Crafts.

LUCKY US *by Summer Fullerton.* **Supplies** *Cardstock:* Prism Papers; *Patterned paper:* A2Z Essentials, Bo-Bunny Press, CherryArte and Scenic Route; *Stickers:* Creative Imaginations; *Chipboard letters:* American Crafts; *Glaze:* Plaid Enterprises; *Chipboard circle:* Imagination Project; *Decorative-edge scissors:* Fiskars; *Font:* Avant Garde, Internet.

SLIDE INTO SPRINGTIME *by Amanda Probst.* **Supplies** *Cardstock:* Prism Papers; *Chipboard letters:* Li'l Davis Designs; *Button:* foof-a-La, Autumn Leaves; *Stamp:* Hero Arts; *Ink:* ColorBox, Clearsnap; *Pen:* Precision Pen, American Crafts.

LOVE YOU *by Laura Kurz.* **Supplies** *Patterned paper:* Scenic Route; *Tag:* Making Memories; *Chipboard letter:* Heidi Swapp for Advantus; "Love You" sticker: Creative Imaginations; *Pin:* Heidi Grace Designs; *Font:* Century Gothic, Microsoft.

"CHINESE GOOD FORTUNE (FU)" FRAME *by Tracey Odachowski.* **Supplies** *Cardstock:* Stampin' Up!; *Metallic paper:* Club Scrap; *Patterned transparency:* Hambly Studios; *Embossing powder:* Stampendous!; *Ink:* VersaMark, Tsukineko; *Frame:* Target.

APRIL

APRIL *by Amanda Probst.* **Supplies** *Cardstock:* Prism Papers; *Vellum:* The Paper Company; *Metal word plates:* Making Memories; *Chipboard letters:* American Crafts; *Fonts:* Century Gothic and Rockwell Extra Bold, Microsoft.

SMUDGE SEASON *by Amanda Probst. Photos by Cassandra Smith.* **Supplies** *Cardstock:* Prism Papers; *Chalk pencils:* Gioconda, Koh-I-Noor; *Fonts:* CK Little Al, www.scrapnfonts.com; Tahoma, Microsoft.

START OF SPRING *by Amanda Probst.* **Supplies** *Cardstock:* Prism Papers; *Chipboard stars:* Li'l Davis Designs; *Pens:* Precision Pen, American Crafts; Artist (red), Marvy Uchida; *Font:* Rockwell, Microsoft.

WHAT PUDDLES R FOR *by Amanda Probst.* **Supplies** *Cardstock:* Prism Papers; *Patterned paper:* My Mind's Eye; *Stamps:* FontWerks; *Ink:* ColorBox, Clearsnap; *Pen:* Gelly Roll Glaze (clear), Sakura; *Font:* CK Jessica, www.scrapnfonts.com; *Other:* Mica.

BASEBALL *by Summer Fullerton.* **Supplies** *Cardstock:* Bazzill Basics Paper; *Patterned paper:* Arctic Frog; *Twill:* Creative Imaginations; *Chipboard letters:* Heidi Swapp for Advantus; *Chipboard shape:* American Crafts; *Metal star:* Queen & Co.; *Font:* Century Gothic, Microsoft.

METAMORPHOSIS *by Amanda Probst.* **Supplies** *Cardstock:* Prism Papers; *Patterned paper:* Making Memories; *Ink:* VersaMark, Tsukineko; *Embossing powder:* Ranger Industries; *Fonts:* LD Painter's Hand, www.scrapnfonts.com; Century Gothic, Microsoft.

SPRING CLEANING *by Tracey Odachowski.* **Supplies** *Cardstock:* Prism Papers (green metallic) and Stampin' Up! (peach); *Patterned paper:* SEI; *Pens:* Sharpie (white), Sanford; Stampin' Up! (brown); *Fonts:* Fling and Fling Alternate letters (title), www.fontshop.com; Garton, www.searchfreefonts.com; *Other:* Vellum.

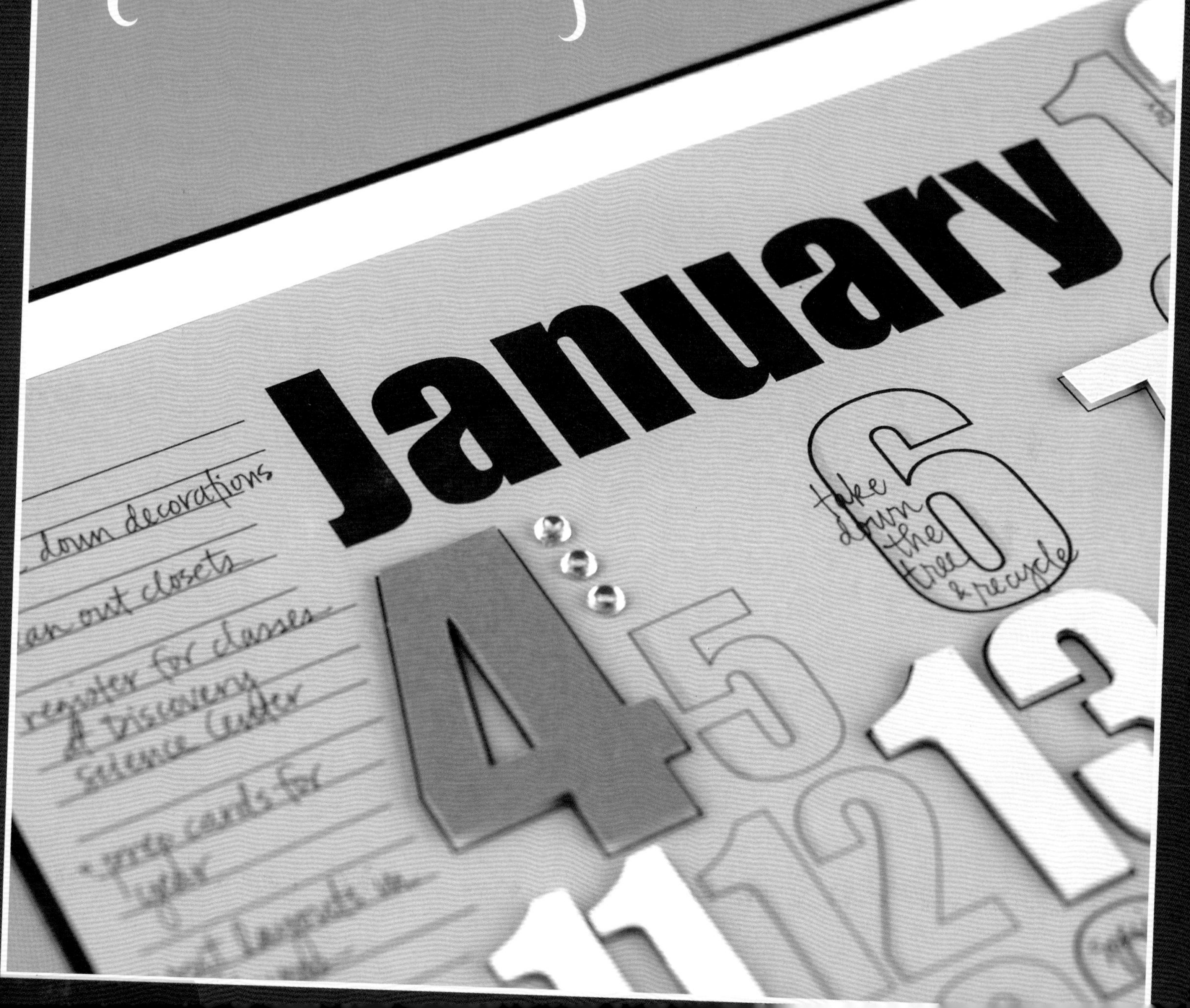

January

...down decorations

...an out closets

...register for classes
A Discovery
Science Center

*prep cards for

take
down
the
tree
& recycle

4

5

6

7

11

12

13

{ SUPPLIES }

JANUARY

BEGINNINGS. January is all about new beginnings. It's an opportunity to reevaluate your priorities, your schedule and even yourself. In the heart of winter, it's a perfect time for staying inside and reflecting, for gearing up for the year to come. My husband and I were actually married on New Year's Eve so we could begin the new year together. Each January, we sit down and plan the year to come, looking forward with anticipation. It's such an awesome opportunity for intention and growth. What do you do to celebrate January?

"LIVE THE LIFE YOU HAVE IMAGINED."
—*Henry David Thoreau*

DECEMBER **journaling** and **photography** PROMPTS

DATE	JOURNALING JUMPSTARTS	PHOTO OPS
December 4: National Cookie Day	What's your favorite cookie and why?	Stacks of cookies Cookie ingredients
December 21: First Day of Winter	What are your best winter memories?	Snow Winter coats Mittens
December 24: Christmas Eve	Write about your family's Christmas Eve traditions.	Holiday decorations Christmas Eve dinner
December 25: Christmas	What's on your holiday wish list?	Shopping Santa Gift wrap
December 31: New Year's Eve	Describe how you ring in the new year.	Clinking of wine glasses Champagne bottles
December: National Stress-Free Family Holiday Month	How do you stay relaxed so you can enjoy the holidays? What things make you happy?	Your family relaxing together

goals:
- take down decorations
- clean out closets
- register for classes at Discovery Science Center
- prep cards for year
- put layouts in albums
- plan meals
- renew annual memberships
- schedule special nights with boys
- start saving for vacation
- laugh more!

January

1 New Year's Day
2
3
4
5
6 take down the tree & recycle
7
8 Mom's b'day
9
10
11
12
13
14
15 Zach & Macey
16
17
18 MLK Jr. day
19
20
21
22
23
24
25 call Nessa
26
27
28 Discovery Science Center @ 11:00 am
29
30 co-op @ 1:00 pm
31

Live the life you have imagined...
-Henry David Thoreau

JANUARY
by Amanda Probst

Make a list.
I don't know about you, but I always seem to need an extra column on my calendar to jot down things that don't fall on a given day. Life gets so crazy, I tend to think in terms of what I need to do during the week or the month to allow myself more flexibility. No doubt your life is busy too. Amid all the craziness, don't forget to live each day with intention.

Monthly Info:
Birthstone: Garnet
Flowers: Carnation, Snowdrop
Astrological signs: Capricorn (Dec. 22–Jan. 19), Aquarius (Jan. 20–Feb. 18)

Save bits and pieces.

Laura made this mini album to preserve remnants of the Christmas season—stamps, ribbon, bits of wrapping paper. For someone who delights in these little touches, this quick reminder will truly be cherished.

AH, THE START OF THE NEW YEAR. WHEN I THINK OF NEW YEARS CELEBRATIONS, I REMEMBER TWO THINGS. ON NEW YEAR'S EVE, WE WERE OFTEN UP AT MY AUNT & UNCLE'S ON HORSE HEAVEN. MY DAD'S FAMILY WOULD GATHER FOR CARD TOURNAMENTS (PINOCHLE IN PARTICULAR), CHATTING AND MAKING PREDICTIONS. WE WOULD WRITE DOWN ALL SORTS OF PREDICTIONS AND MY AUNT WOULD STORE THEM AWAY...TO BE OPENED AND READ THE FOLLOWING YEAR. PREDICTIONS RANGED FROM GUESSED AT RELATIONSHIP TURNS TO WHAT YOU'D BE WEARING WHEN YOU OPENED THE PREDICTION THE FOLLOWING YEAR. SILLY, REALLY, BUT VERY FUN.

ON NEW YEAR'S DAY, WE'D SWITCH TO MY MOM'S SIDE OF THE FAMILY. I REMEMBER GOING TO MY GRANDPARENTS' HOUSE IN UNION GAP...GETTING TOGETHER TO EAT AND SOMETIMES EVEN WEAR THE SPARKLY HATS. I REMEMBER, THOUGH, NEVER BEING FULLY AT EASE IN MY GRANDPARENTS' HOUSE. THERE WERE SO MANY THINGS WE WEREN'T ALLOWED TO TOUCH. PLUS, WE JUST WEREN'T AS CLOSE TO MY MOM'S SIDE OF THE FAMILY... SEEING THEM LESS FREQUENTLY THAN MY DAD'S FAMILY AND HAVING CONSIDERABLY FEWER FIRST COUSINS (AND ALMOST ALL OF THEM WERE OLDER AND NOT INTERESTED IN THE SAME THINGS WE WERE). SO, WE AMUSED OURSELVES FOR THE MOST PART DURING SUCH FAMILY GATHERINGS. STILL, THE FOOD WAS GREAT.

eve & day

{ EVE & DAY }
by Amanda Probst

Remember your childhood.

I get overwhelmed when I consider all the childhood memories I want to record. So, I'm taking it one month at a time. Here, I tell the story of what I remember about celebrating New Year's Eve and New Year's Day growing up. Instead of focusing on specific happenings, I recorded the more general routine of these holidays.

In our house, Christmas is a year-round celebration.

It started years ago when we attended the Fiftieth Anniversary celebration at the Senator Theater. It continued when Chris gave me the movie poster with the tickets from that evening for our first married Christmas together. Then, a few years later, we gave each other the same gift – an ornament. We have three of those now, and one stays on the mantel throughout the year. Of course, when it was time to name a dog, the last member of our family, what better name for her than 'Zuzu.'

This is our everyday Christmas. It makes the holidays even more special for us each year.

It's a Wonderful Life, isn't it?

{ OUR WONDERFUL LIFE }

by Tracey Odachowski

Describe a favorite holiday movie.

Tracey's family has a particular fondness for the movie *It's a Wonderful Life*, which she documented here. My family used to watch *The Wizard of Oz* every December. What did you watch during the month of December when you were growing up? Do you have any holiday shows that have sparked collections?

NOTE TO SELF

DATE: *jan 1*

RE: *fresh starts*

CC:

Januarys. They just don't get much fan fare these days. We haven't attended a New Year's Eve party in ages. Generally, you can find us sitting at home, perhaps with some sparkling cider, playing games until midnight…not hugely unlike most days for us. We watch the NYC Times Square ceremony announcing the new year, toast each other and continue as usual. We rarely do anything more exciting than hanging around the house on New Year's Day. As the month progresses, we take down holiday decorations, try to remember to recycle the tree before the City's free recycling closes up, and gear up for the new year. We generally spend and do less, as we recuperate from the holidays. Not too exciting, eh?

But. January is also the month we tend to sit down and map out a "plan" for the coming year. There's just something special about starting points, don't you think? I love the wonderful opportunity that they provide…to recreate yourself and your life. It doesn't have to be anything huge; often the smallest intentions are the most worthwhile. January is a time for taking stock and making notes to yourself for the future. So. Yes, I make resolutions and goals each year, each January. This layout, though, is not about those goals. Instead, it is about the power found in *making* the goals…delighting in the possibilities that fresh starts provide. Rather than view Januarys only as those dreary winter months for recovering from the holidays (which, undeniably, they are), I choose to see the incredible potential… to recognize the power to be had in making intentions. Remember that.

☒ RECEIVED BY SELF

"CORRESPONDENCE WITH SOMEONE YOU LOVE"

NOTE TO SELF
by Amanda Probst

Delve deeper than making goals.
Making goals is wonderful. I do it all the time. But, beyond recording what those goals are and when you meet them, take a moment to consider just how powerful the act of making goals is.

Some days you just have to shake your head and resign yourself to the fact that you're the mother of three boys. Maybe it's just the fact that the snow is keeping us indoors and they have serious cabin fever. Maybe it's just what boys do. Either way, they LOVE to race their dump trucks around the family room at top speeds as I cringe and hope for a collision free night. Lately, they've taken to launching their dump trucks over the steps from the hallway to the family room as well. Micah has joined in this activity wholeheartedly, using his shopping cart since we have yet to find a matching dump truck for him. He doesn't seem to mind. He just thrills in joining his big brothers in their rough and tumble ways. Meanwhile, I try to stay out of the way and hope for the best...all the while grinning and thinking to myself that girls wouldn't do this.

GIRLS WOULDN'T DO THAT

{ GIRLS WOULDN'T DO THAT }
by Amanda Probst

Photograph cabin fever.

"In the middle of winter, when our family spends more time indoors, the boys need another outlet for their energy. Last winter, they raced their dump trucks around the family room. I distinctly remember shaking my head and thinking, "girls wouldn't do that!" Thus a layout was born.

These snowball makers were a big hit, having been added to our arsenal the night before the big snow. While Noah promptly took up snowball fights, Asher delighted more in the act of simply making the snowballs…apparently receiving some sense of satisfaction in creating such nice round balls.

snow ball maker

{ SNOWBALL MAKER }

by Amanda Probst

Use bright colors.

So many snow and winter layouts end up with colors like white, blue and silver or gray. (Heck, aside from the hat, check out what my son is wearing.) When Asher received this wonderful hand-knit hat from his grandma, I knew I wouldn't lack for color in my photos this winter. Using it as my inspiration, I went bold with the colors on this page and ended up with a fun and upbeat layout—happy, just like the day was.

{ YOUR STORY }
by Summer Fullerton

Attach homework.

Summer tucked away this class assignment (to describe a Christmas tradition) by her son and used it with pictures of the following year. We both love how beautifully it turned out and how much more touching the story is in her son's own words.

miD niGhT KisSeS

Yes, you actually stayed up until midnight. Call us bad parents for letting a 2-year-old stay up that late, but we had a good excuse. It was New Year's Eve, after all, and you were being a very good little girl all evening! You loved helping me roll the dice in Yahtzee and cuddling with Mommom Sissy. So, we let you stay up and have a little bubbly (aka. Sprite) when the ball dropped. Lucky me, I even got a kiss from my favorite little girl at midnight. For that, it was worth bending all parenting rules for an evening.   New Year 2007

{ MIDNIGHT KISSES }
by Tracey Odachowski

Be inspired by a clock.

I love how Tracey used a clock face here! She created the numbers using die cuts as masks and added her own clock hands. The entire design ties in so nicely with the story and the title of the page. I definitely see myself scraplifting this in the future!

12-25-86

Dear Amanda,

This is my stamp collection book that I had when I was your age. In it are some stamps that I had collected, but there is still room for many more. Stamp collecting can be a very fun hobby. There are other sources where you can get stamps, at special stores, letters and the U.S. Post Office. Take care of this collection, add to it and have fun.

Merry Christmas

Dad

Think back for a moment, would you? Do you have a particular Christmas gift that you received as a child that you still remember? That you possibly even still have? I tried this and can honestly only remember one gift distinctly. The others are a bit of a blur.

The one gift I remember is my dad's stamp collection. He gave it to me when I was eleven and included this note. The fact that my dad actually took the time to write a note and knew what was in the present, itself, was significant. The fact that he would share something so treasured was even more so. My dad is a fairly private and quiet sort of guy, so this glimpse into his life was a rare treat, something that truly made an impression. Did I take up stamp collecting myself? For awhile. Do I still have and treasure this collection? You betchya! I haven't added anything to it in years, but I do hope to one day get it all organized so I can share it with my sons. It remains one of my favorite gifts of all time.

So. Thinking about all this, I've been considering whether the gifts we're giving our sons are ones they'll remember. I hope some of them are. I know now that I'll be more aware of this in the future. Here's to gifts...

WORTH REMEMBERING

Include a handwritten note.

What were some of your favorite gifts you received growing up? This note, by itself, was significant to me—significant because my dad took the time to write it and because it was intended to be passed along with a treasured collection. Here, I focused on the note but also included photos from the collection and actual stamps.

This year we set a goal to have dedicated one-on-one time with each boy. We've been trying to do it weekly, but with three boys it turns out to be an odd rotation. (So, for example, Noah and Nathan on Tuesday...Asher and me on Thursday...Micah and Nathan on Tuesday...Noah and me on Thursday...) We call them

SPECIAL NIGHTS

Often, it's nothing more than heading to Barnes & Noble and reading some books together before getting drinks at Starbucks and heading home again (with a couple extra drinks for the boys at home of course). Sometimes we also get dinner together or do something altogether different that we've planned ahead of time with that night's boy. The important thing, though, is the one-on-one time...the opportunity to really listen to that boy and just be together. Now and again, we've had to take breaks from Special Nights for various reasons, but they continue to be a definite part of our lives...something we know it's important to make time for.

{ SPECIAL NIGHTS }
by Amanda Probst

Make a date with your child.

Last year, as part of our new year's plan, we decided to have "special nights" with each of our boys—some one-on-one time on a regular basis. This opportunity to spend quality time with each child has been wonderful and was a terrific way to start our year.

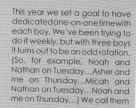

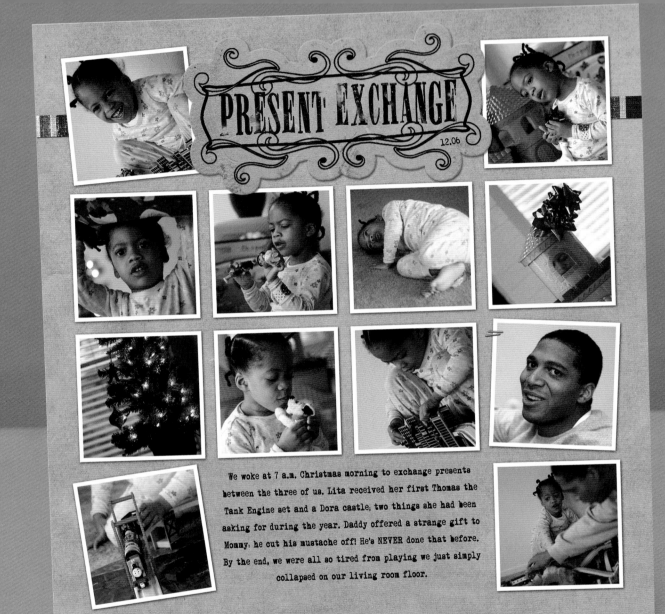

PRESENT EXCHANGE

12.06

We woke at 7 a.m. Christmas morning to exchange presents between the three of us. Lita received her first Thomas the Tank Engine set and a Dora castle; two things she had been asking for during the year. Daddy offered a strange gift to Mommy: he cut his mustache off! He's NEVER done that before. By the end, we were all so tired from playing we just simply collapsed on our living room floor.

{ PRESENT EXCHANGE }

by Tiffany Tillman

Take snapshots.

The obligatory Christmas-morning photos. We all have them. To add interest to her layout, Tiffany matted each photo, creating the feel of quick, little snapshots. Here, then, is her story via 12 little glimpses. Perfect.

In 2007, we will renovate our bathrooms.

We will replace our 1940s tile with new, vintage tile.

We will have toilet seats that don't fall off.

We will have a new-looking porcelin tub.

We will have shower heads that function properly.

We will have sinks that don't look dirty after one use.

WE WANT
WE LOVE
WE WORK
WE LIKE
WE DREAM
WE LIVE

We will have baths that fit the rest of our updated house.

We will save the money to make this happen, and more.

We will

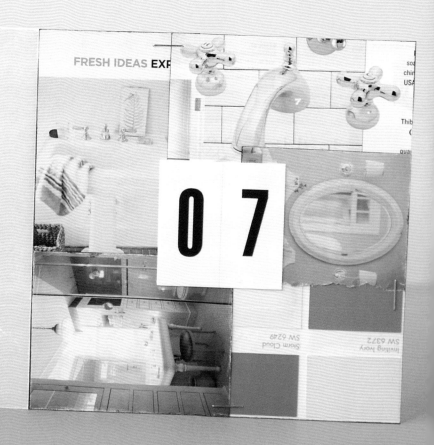

WE WILL
by Laura Kurz

Rip ideas from magazines.

Laura added snippets she'd ripped from magazines and catalogs to the right-hand page of her layout to show ideas for renovating her bathrooms. If you draw your inspiration from another source, why not include it on your layout?

It started snowing on Wednesday and we were finally able to get out the door on Saturday (after extensive shoveling). Noah wasn't deterred in the least by the 24 inches or so of snow and set off quickly to make snowball hoards and attack us. Given his light weight, he managed to not sink into the snow quite as much as Nathan and I so was able to run away fairly well. While his brothers stayed near the edges of the yard contentedly playing with the snow, Noah traversed the yard, tried to bury Nathan and generally just had great fun.

{ YAY 4 SNOW }
by Amanda Probst

Group your photos.

If it's not obvious, I love to group my photos. Here, I used two separate groupings, but notice how they look like one larger unit thanks to the placement of my title and journaling. I love how this technique allows me to fit several pictures on one page without a cluttered look.

ONCE I DIDNT LIKE TO HAVE *my picture* TAKEN.

NOW IM MAKING IT A POINT TO DO SO.

HOPEFULLY LATER SOMEONE WILL THINK THIS IS A good THING...

me

Get out from behind the camera.

We're all guilty. We end up behind the camera way more often than we're in front of it. But years from now, our loved ones will want to see pictures of us, too. So, even if you're like me and truly prefer to avoid being in pictures, make sure to hand off that camera every now and again. It'll be worth it!

{ ME }
by Amanda Probst

PRESENT

I didn't realize it until we moved to Colorado. It was the first time Nathan was working full time in a job with actual "hours" during December since we'd been married. (Prior to that, he'd done odd jobs or been self-employed or been at a job where he made his own hours.) He couldn't just take time off whenever he wanted and wasn't able to join us to celebrate Christmas until Christmas Eve Mass. This bothered me and I couldn't figure out why. Then I realized, Growing up, my dad was always around more in the winter, especially around Christmas...always more present. The farm work didn't demand nearly as much time, so he was on hand to bake and watch football with us and just be there whenever we decided to do something holiday related. Not having Nathan on hand like that seemed wrong, though I didn't understand why. Once I realized, I've worked at coming to terms with the fact that most dads don't have as much available time in December as mine did growing up. I still don't particularly like it, but I understand. So, now, when I see Nathan reading with the boys or helping with the tree or playing in the snow, I appreciate that all the more.

PRESENT
by Amanda Probst

Compare past and present.

A couple of years ago, I came to a realization about the month of December. I realized I had carried my expectations from Christmas traditions and celebrations in my childhood over to my own family. I recognized that the situations are different and require different expectations. This light-bulb moment helped me adjust my outlook.

We always said when we started putting up Christmas lights on the outside of our house we wouldn't be one of those people who leave them up for six months. So here we are in the frigid cold making good on our promise. I find it funny how it seems like it took days to put up the lights but only hours to take them down. The work is always worth it when I turn the corner to our house and the lights are twinkling and the kids get excited. I admit I get a little excited too. Good-bye lights until we meet again next year.

bye

{ BYE }
by Summer Fullerton

Photograph the mundane.

Raise your hand if you've taken pictures of you and your family putting up holiday decorations. Now raise your hand if you've ever taken pictures of taking them *down*. Yup. Me neither. I hereby resolve to do so, because I think it's a valuable part of the entire story.

Funny. Though my boys (and most kids, I'd guess) seem to think Christmas revolves around the gifts, I don't remember many specific gifts I received at Christmas as a kid. What I DO remember is baking with my dad... getting a tree at the U-cut place down the road...watching my dad put up the outside lights...decorating the house inside with garlands and lights and everything else... the mistletoe ball my mom loves (it was my dad's dad's)... the stockings my godmother made for us...the beautiful nativity my mom always set out...Christmas Eve children's Mass with kids acting out the nativity story...watching out the window for Rudolph on the way home from church... taking a group photo in our Christmas Eve finery... opening one or two presents Christmas Eve, always one of them being new pajamas...listening to Christmas music all month long...and so much more. I hope my boys have similar fond memories and I try to remember this when Christmas craziness looms.

Santa
SEASON WEAR

DO YOU BELIEVE?

the PHOTO

{ THE PHOTO }
by Amanda Probst

List your memories.

Christmastime brings back so many memories for me that trying to write about them cohesively was a challenge. Instead, I opted just to list them. For this layout, I picked one memory to highlight and found a photo to match.

by Tiffany Tillman

Jot your notes some-place pretty.

Tiffany made these gorgeous journaling cards for the year. Her plan is to write her goals/wishes/ hopes/thoughts at the beginning of each month. Notice how each card is decorated and tabbed to reflect that particular month.

DEC

1
2 Dad's birthday
4 co-op 1pm
recital @ 2:30pm
12

Special Night Nathan & Noah

get & decorate tree
6 7 8 9 enjoy laughter delight

happiness

haircuts for boys~
Joy & Peace
NCHA mtg @ 7pm
14
Date night 7pm
17 18 caroling
John & Nancy arriving

cookie exchange deadline for church giving tree
20
first snow of winter
23 call Molly
25 Christmas

30 31 our anniversary

by Amanda Probst

DECEMBER

Deck the calendar with lengths of ribbon.

Inspired by gift wrap, I designed this calendar using ribbon as the lines for my page (adding a slight tilt just for kicks). I think the result is a very festive calendar.

Monthly Info:

Birthstone: Turquoise
Flower: Narcissus
Astrological signs: Sagittarius (Nov. 22–Dec. 21), Capricorn (Dec. 22–Jan. 19)

JANUARY **journaling** and **photography** PROMPTS

DATE	JOURNALING JUMPSTARTS	PHOTO OPS
January 1: New Year's Day	How do you celebrate the new year?	A new year's toast A purchase you made to help meet this year's resolutions (like an exercise bike)
January 6: Epiphany/ Three Kings Day	As a child, we tried to leave our tree up until Epiphany. What's your process for taking down your tree?	Taking down the tree Your room after the tree has been removed
January 11: Amelia Earhart Day	How has being a woman affected your life?	A brave woman in your life You trying something new
January 17: Benjamin Franklin's Birthday	Are you thrifty or a spender?	A jar full of change Your local bank
January 18: A. A. Milne's Birthday	Which Winnie the Pooh character do you have the most in common with?	A favorite childhood book A stuffed animal or toy character
Third Monday of January: Martin Luther King, Jr. Day	Do you have a dream? What is it?	Something that represents your dream

DECEMBER

CELEBRATION. Whew! December is the end of a busy year. It's all about celebrating—celebrating the holiday of your choice, celebrating the onset of winter, celebrating time together as a family. As winter sets in, we stay home more and turn to indoor activities to occupy us. Make sure at least some of those activities bring you together with loved ones.

"NOT **EVERYTHING** THAT CAN BE COUNTED COUNTS, AND NOT EVERYTHING **THAT COUNTS** CAN BE COUNTED."

—*Albert Einstein*

FEBRUARY

LOVE. It's February, and love is in the air. From hearts and flowers to chocolates and love letters, February is all about affection. This month, don't just celebrate the love of your life; remember the simple things you love too, like your favorite book or your favorite food. Warm up the chilly days of February by focusing on all the things you love!

"REMEMBER THIS: ANY **WORD** YOU SPEAK WITH **MEANING** WILL HAVE **POWER.**"
—*Ernest Holmes*

NOVEMBER journaling and photography PROMPTS

DATE	JOURNALING JUMPSTARTS	PHOTO OPS
November 3: National Sandwich Day	What's your favorite sandwich?	Sandwich ingredients Your favorite sandwich Sandwich restaurants
November 7: National Magazine Day	What magazines do you love to read and why?	A shot re-created from a photo you love in a magazine Magazines you receive in the mail
First Tuesday of November: Election Day	Write about your voting experiences.	Campaign signs Voter registration Lines of voters
Fourth Thursday of November: Thanksgiving	How does your family celebrate Thanksgiving?	Thanksgiving feast Table settings Food traditions
November 11: Veterans' Day	Write about a friend or family member who served in the military.	Members of the military Uniforms Insignia
November 30: Stay at Home Because You're Well Day	How would you spend a "free" day at home?	Activities during your day at home Clothes you'd wear on a lazy day at home Food you like to eat on a day off

february

1.
groundhog day 2.
3.
4.
5.
co-op @ 1 pm 6.
7.

work on Valentines... 8.
9.
10.
11.
12.
13.

15.
Presidents day 16.
mail package to Prosser 17.
18.
special night me & Asher 19.
20.
21.

HAYLEE 22.
23.
24.
Ash Wed. 25.
library books due! 26.
27.
28.

{ FEBRUARY }
by Amanda Probst

Make your own box of chocolates.
Inspired by a box of chocolates, I made this calendar to share the hidden delights in every day.

Monthly Info:
Birthstone: Amethyst
Flower: Violet
Astrological signs: Aquarius (Jan. 20–Feb. 18), Pisces (Feb. 19–Mar. 20)

{ GRATITUDE JOURNAL }
by Amanda Probst

Count your blessings.

This is just a simple three-ring journal for jotting down things I'm thankful for. My plan is to add a new page with journaling or a photo each day during the month of November, so I'll have a nice little album by Thanksgiving. I'm going to make one for each of my boys as well; inside, they can draw pictures of what they're thankful for each day.

424

2

FEBRUARYS

I don't have any specific childhood memories of Valentine's Day. Wait. I do remember all the little Valentines exchanged during school...making special mailboxes and writing out cards for classmates. Nothing spectacular, but I suppose it was a nice excuse to have some candy, and I did enjoy making those art projects. I never was one of those girls very into pink and frills and hearts, though, so Valentine's Day has just never appealed to me much. Before Nathan, I don't know that I was ever even dating during Valentine's so I missed out on that aspect of it as well. I guess the best that can be said of Valentine's Day is that it managed to bring a little excitement to our otherwise fairly sedate Februarys. Come to think of it, Februarys really were pretty empty of events...between sports seasons, after end/ start of terms...no reliable reason to be busy. Guess there have to be months like that.

{ FEBRUARYS }
by Amanda Probst

Tell a story, even if there's not much to tell.

Okay, this isn't the most exciting layout ever. The important thing, though, is that I wrote down how I felt about the month of February growing up. It's part of the larger picture of my childhood. For me, some months just weren't as exciting as others. But if I didn't say so, future generations wouldn't know I felt that way—they might just think I was missing those layouts!

I think dogs are the most amazing creatures; they give unconditional love. For me they are the role model for being alive. *Gilda Radnor*

{ UNCONDITIONAL LOVE }
by Laura Kurz

Keep it simple.

While you're reflecting on what you're thankful for this Thanksgiving season, don't forget the pets in your life. Laura found this quote that perfectly echoed her thoughts. Simple and true.

To my sweet boys...
This Valentine's Day I sat & watched you enjoying the party. I was so proud of you for reading your own Valentine's cards before the party & always love to see you create as you did when you made your "mailboxes" for Valentines. I was prouder still when you overcame your usual shyness to participate in the relay races & other games. Seeing you sit patiently and decorate your Valentine's cupcakes, I realized that Valentine's is no longer about romance for me. These days, it's about watching you celebrate. I see you learning to give of yourselves & look forward to teaching you about the art of giving gifts to girls (years down the road, right?). You are my reason to observe this holiday. So, this Valentine's Day I just wanted to tell you that I love you all.
You are my Valentines...
                                        Love,
                                          mommy

You're mine

{ YOU'RE MINE }
by Amanda Probst

Write a love letter.
It doesn't have to be a mushy love letter, but write one. This one is to my boys, describing how they've influenced my perspective on Valentine's Day.

I'd never really given it much thought growing up. In my home, it felt like there was just always food in the kitchen; and, since I wasn't responsible for feeding everyone, I didn't fully appreciate what that meant. Now that I *am* responsible for feeding my family, I can truly savor one of the oft forgotten things to be thankful for at Thanksgiving...the leftovers. Look at that fridge, just full of good food...meals I won't have to think up or plan or make. How incredibly awesome. I seriously love leftovers.

thank **full**

{ THANK FULL }
by Amanda Probst

Appreciate the little things.
Leftovers. I love 'em. While we take plenty of pictures of Thanksgiving feasts, how many of us take pictures of the refrigerator the day after?

Look at these two pictures. They were taken the same day. Both are of my dad's parents on their wedding day. Both show them in their finery. Is it just me, though, or is the one on the right way more fun? Sure, I understand and appreciate formal portraits, but the candid shot speaks volumes to me. It gives me a peek into my grandparents' life and the kind of people they were. It reminds me that those are the types of shots that my own children and grandchildren will someday cherish. I hope Nathan & I look as happy and engaging as these two.

{ THEN & THEN }
by Amanda Probst

Compare and contrast.

I found these two old pictures of my dad's parents on their wedding day and was torn by which to include on my layout. I thought I only wanted to use one to portray the day, but then I realized that together they tell their own story. I love how my layout turned out and have to credit my husband for coming up with the title!

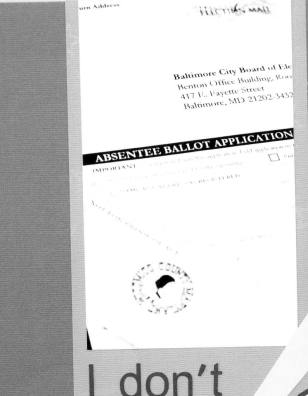

Go ahead. Lecture me about how I am not fulfilling my civic duty. I can handle it. But I have my reasons. In fact, no one in this house votes. It's not that we don't feel that we should; on the contrary, every election season we remind ourselves how much we need to. Yet, as the election process carries forth, we get disgusted. Tired of the backstabbing commercials. Fed up with constant election coverage. So, by the time the first Tuesday in November rolls around, there is absolutely no one on the ballot that we feel actually deserves two votes. It's terrible, I know, but that's the way it is. And don't getting me started on hanging chads. Now, if you put Colin Powell on a ballot, you just might find us in a booth. Of course, that is the second problem. We're registered in Maryland, yet we haven't lived there for years. We're a military family, and we just can't change our licenses every time we move. I've never felt very comfortable trying to decide who to vote for in Maryland because it has very little impact on us. Did I mention that my voter registration actually still has my maiden name on it? Yeah, it's that old. I'm just not motivated to change it. Maybe things will change next year. Chris will be out of the Army, and we'll be forced to become Virginia residents. Suddenly, even local elections will affect us. Then maybe we'll vote. (Although, I wouldn't place any bets on it.)

I don't vote

{ I DON'T VOTE } by Tracey Odachowski

Vote, or don't.

November means Thanksgiving feasts and early Christmas shopping, but it also means elections. I love Tracey's admission that she doesn't vote. I love her rationale. What are your thoughts?

one boy

we played this song at our rehearsal
seven years later it's still true we are still one boy
one girl a little older a little more in love

one girl

{ ONE BOY,
ONE GIRL }
by Laura Kurz

Use a song as inspiration.

Laura used the song played at her wedding rehearsal years ago as the starting point for this page. Isn't it amazing how a simple song can trigger so many memories and warm fuzzies? I also love how this transparency page is two-sided so that when it's slipped into a page protector, it's already complete on both sides.

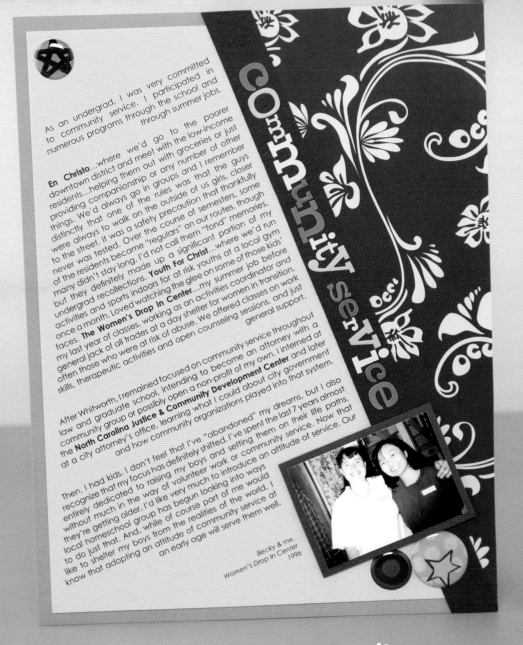

community service

As an undergrad, I was very committed to community service. I participated in numerous programs through the school and through summer jobs.

En Christo...where we'd go to the poorer downtown district and meet with the low-income residents...helping them out with groceries or just providing companionship or any number of other things. We'd always go in groups and I remember distinctly that one of the rules was that the guys were always to walk on the outside of us girls, closer to the street. It was a safety precaution that thankfully never was tested. Over the course of semesters, some of the residents became "regulars" on our routes, though many didn't stay long. I'd not call them "fond" memories, but they definitely made up a significant portion of my undergrad recollections. **Youth For Christ**...where we'd run activities and sports indoors for at risk youths at a local gym once a month. Loved watching the glee on some of those kids' faces. **The Women's Drop In Center**...my summer job before my last year of classes, working as an activities coordinator and general jack of all trades at a day shelter for women in transition, often those who were at risk of abuse. We offered classes on work skills, therapeutic activities and open counseling sessions, and just general support.

After Whitworth, I remained focused on community service throughout law and graduate school, intending to become an attorney with a community group or possibly open a non-profit of my own. I interned at the **North Carolina Justice & Community Development Center** and later at a city attorney's office, learning what I could about city government and how community organizations played into that system.

Then, I had kids. I don't feel that I've "abandoned" my dreams, but I also recognize that my focus has definitely shifted. I've spent the last 7 years almost entirely dedicated to raising my boys and setting them on their life paths, without much in the way of volunteer work or community service. Now that they're getting older, I'd like very much to introduce an attitude of service. Our local homeschool group has begun looking into ways to do just that. And, while of course part of me would like to shelter my boys from the realities of the world, I know that adopting an attitude of community service at an early age will serve them well.

Becky & me,
Women's Drop In Center
1996

{ COMMUNITY SERVICE }
by Amanda Probst

Serve your community.

Once upon a time, I did a much better job of serving my community. Today, my contribution comes mainly from raising good citizens. Though community service is needed all year long, just before the holidays is a common time to contemplate such goodwill. What sorts of community service do you do? What do you hope to do?

Such simple things, but words carry mighty weight. They are important. Just as those three little words "I LOVE YOU" convey so much, bedtime routines can also show how much you care. In our home, Nathan is generally in charge of bedtimes. He gets the boys "last calls" (a last chance to eat so that they don't wake partially through the night and come to us claiming to be hungry), puts them in pajamas, brushes teeth, reads or plays a game, refills water cups (that just stay by each boys' bed, again to prevent any delay tactics) and then sends them to me. My job is to give them a hug and say goodnights. It goes like this. They say to me, "everything to say goodnights...everything back to you." (They say it all in one breath, the second portion being in response to anything I might say but it's become so much a part of things that they now get it out before I even have a chance to say anything.) Then, in addition to any personal notes from the day or in anticipation of tomorrow, I say "Have good sleep and good dreams...I'll see you in the morning...I love you." Nothing fancy. Just our thing. But leave out even one part of it, and it's just not the same. In fact, Asher's been known to get out of bed and come get me just so I can tell him to have good dreams. He claims he won't if I don't tell him to. Ah, the power of words.

THE POWER OF WORDS

by Amanda Probst

Pay attention to your words.

In our home, we try to be careful with our words, not making idle threats or saying things unless we truly mean them. I remember as a teenager refusing to tell boyfriends I loved them—I wanted to reserve those words for the special people in my life. Do you have special words you use regularly?

GIVE THANKS

count your blessings • count your blessings • count your blessings • count your blessings • count your blessings • count your blessings • count your blessings •

Thanksgiving dinner was hand delivered to our house by Grandma and Grandpa. It traveled comfortably in their car for several hours though the desert and over the mountain all because I cannot cook a turkey. Originally we were supposed to go to Bend for the holiday. Grandma had ordered Thanksgiving dinner from Wild Oats and it was scheduled to be a stress free no-cook holiday. But the weather turned cold and icy and it was decided that since we don't have 4-wheel drive they would come to us instead. So Grandma picked up our pre-cooked dinner and drove it from Bend to our house. My visions of a no-cook Thanksgiving dinner quickly faded away. Don't get me wrong I love the idea of Thanksgiving; spending time with my family enjoying a good meal and laughing. But I don't love the hours of standing in the kitchen cooking and cleaning. And quite frankly our family consists of too many picky eaters (point in case note the plate of meatloaf on Grandpa's plate) for us to go to all this trouble. I know I am not alone when I say this but can we please just go out to dinner next year.

nov 2006

GIVE THANKS
by Summer Fullerton

Be honest.

You probably can't tell at first glance that this is a layout about how much Summer dislikes cooking on Thanksgiving. It is. By using goofy pictures of her family and adding the beautifully hand-cut leaf accents in bright colors, Summer managed to turn this into a warm and inviting layout—one with a sense of humor!

Jinxy: my third Calico kitty. I'm not sure why I'm so attracted to these Tabbies. Always female, sometimes a little feisty, and never as 'luxurious' as some other kittens ...

love

Jinxy will be the third I have owned and raised since kitten-hood. I guess I'm a sucker for the little scamps chewing on my fingertips. One thing for sure: I AM A CAT LOVER. I am.

i do.

sweet

{ JINXY }
by Tiffany Tillman

Celebrate your pets.

Do you have a pet? We, um, have goldfish. Not too exciting, but it's what works for us right now. Tiffany loves calicos, and who can blame her? Look at that adorable little kitty. While thinking of people and things you love this month, don't forget your pets!

Silly me. I thought I was on top of things for a change and tried to take photos for our Christmas card early. Micah had other ideas. Someone please tell me…what's the trick to getting a 15 month old to sit still for a Christmas card photo? Already I was trying to simplify things by having individual pictures rather than trying to get all three boys to cooperate at the same time. I thought that was pretty smart of me. Still, Micah wanted nothing to do with that darn "O" and was even less interested in wearing the Santa hat. I had Noah putting the hat back on Micah's head and Asher propping the "O" back up and both of them jumping out of the way quickly while I tried to capture the millisecond with the camera. That didn't work. We took a little break, during which Micah was more than happy enough to play with the letters. (At one point he kept swiping the "J" while Noah was trying to spell out "Joy" against the wall…which left "oy" which was the perfect word for the afternoon, hence the title here.) In the end, I resorted to bribery. Yes, I gave him Smarties candies to try to get him to sit still…had Noah and Asher still helping with the props. Regardless, this is the best shot we got before we ran out of Smarties. Oy.

{ OY }
by Amanda Probst

Bribe the kid.

November is usually when I start thinking about photos for our holiday cards. This layout documents how difficult it can be to photograph a toddler. In the end, we resorted to bribery—until I ran out of Smarties candies. (Note, also, that I used the sample display sheet that comes with the paper collection for the strips of patterned paper.)

4.29.2007
Today, at age 21 months, Micah ate:

a whole banana
some stoned wheat crackers
shredded wheat cereal (say 1/3 of a bowl that an adult would eat)
2-3 peanut butter cracker sandwich thingies (PB between two crackers)
1/3 of a turkey sandwich
bowl of yogurt
small vanilla ice cream cone from DQ (yes, the whole thing)
another banana
2-3 more peanut butter cracker sandwiches
2 slices of french bread
bowl of leftover ravioli (all that we had... he'd have eaten more)
more peanut butter crackers
another half a banana
most of a package of Ramen noodles (minus the broth)

Seriously. And that's not counting the many snacks and whatnot he finagles from his brothers that I don't always see or all the water and soy milk he drinks. Many days he'll eat an entire bowl of macaroni & cheese or 3 taquitos and then proceed to finish off Noah and Asher's lunches as well. Honest, I don't think the other two combined ate that much at his age. Heck, some days the other two combined don't eat as much now.

a love affair with food

{ A LOVE AFFAIR WITH FOOD }
by Amanda Probst

Scrap a love affair.
Love doesn't just have to be about people. Here I documented my youngest son's rather significant love of food. I jotted down everything he ate in one 24-hour period and snapped some pictures of him chowing down. What sorts of things or activities are you in love with?

Ah, Thanksgiving. One of my favorite holidays growing up. Since moving away and being unable to attend family celebrations, though, we've not had the most spectacular Thanksgivings...too busy or too lazy to do anything special. Heck, most years I have to remind Nathan when it is. This year, though, we decided to do something...anything. We realized that we can't wait around forever for the days when we'll be able to afford to travel home for family Thanksgivings. (Besides, the family Thanksgivings we remember are becoming a thing of the past as cousins grow up and start families of their own.) We need to make an effort now, particularly if we want our boys to have fond Thanksgiving memories like our own. They deserve that. So. This year I made Thanksgiving crafts with the boys ahead of time (paper turkeys)...we read Thanksgiving stories...we made a Thanksgiving meal (okay, we still weren't brave enough to tackle an actual turkey, opting for pot roast instead, but it was a full *meal* with multiple dishes and everything)...we made pies and sugar cookies. Sure, it still wasn't the grand full day I remember growing up, but it was more than just another day. And for that, I am thankful.

4TH THURSDAY OF NOVEMBER
by Amanda Probst

State the obvious.

It can be a challenge to come up with good titles for holiday pages. Sometimes, I find it's easiest to simply state the obvious. In this case, my journaling and page is about Thanksgiving . . . the fourth Thursday of November.

Biltmore

I'm not certain that I can put into words how much we fell in love with this place. When we drove up to it, we were absolutely overwhelmed by the sheer size of it. To think that this house has 4 acres of square footage on 80,000 acres of land but was built for only one man is mind-blowing. Yes, eventually his wife and daughter moved in as well, and a bazillion servants, but still. The horse stalls were bigger and better than our home. I kept finding myself analyzing the intricate details. Oh, and the inside; immaculate and posh in every way. Of course, we weren't allowed to take any photographs indoors, which was upsetting, but it did give me the chance to enjoy it more. I do recall finding it rather funny that everything was so lavishly dressed, but the bathrooms were small with all white tiles. A bit of an oxymoron in today's world, but I have to remind myself that back then having working bathrooms was revolutionary. We toured the home for nearly two hours, yet saw less than half of it. Amazing. I'm so happy that we finally took the time to go to Biltmore, and I cannot wait to go back.

Valentine's Weekend 2007

{ BILTMORE }
by Tracey Odachowski

Capture a favorite place.

If you've never been to the Biltmore Estate in North Carolina, you should go. Seriously. I was so excited when Tracey created this layout about her Valentine's weekend at Biltmore. It's one of my favorite places as well (my husband and I visited it for the first time on a Valentine's weekend too).

Thanksgiving was always my favorite holiday growing up, even more than Christmas. At Thanksgiving, my dad's family would all get together. Often, the gathering would be up at the family farm where my dad and his seven brothers and sisters grew up. (Some years we'd all go to a different location altogether and it became a vacation.) We'd play touch football in the driveway or pasture and then head inside for food (oh, the wonderful and plentiful food!) and pinochle. It was an opportunity to catch up with my 20 cousins, most of whom were also good friends. Sometimes, my aunt Lillian would organize an art project of some sort…Christmas ornaments one year, tablecloth art another year…stuff like that. My dad and his brothers and sisters would have a family meeting at some point (they all run the family farm corporation together). As we got older, trips to the movie theaters weren't uncommon. Basically, it was just a fabulous time with family…so full with the gifts of laughter, friendship and love. I miss that.

bountiful

{ BOUNTIFUL }
by Amanda Probst

Focus on the artwork.
I always loved the pieces of "art" we created at Thanksgivings when I was growing up, so I chose to display them as the dominant photo on this page. The doodles represent a number of my relatives' work. Notice how the warm colors evoke Thanksgiving.

HOW SWEET IT IS . . .
I LOVE THEE . . .
BE MINE

by Summer Fullerton

Make your own valentines.

Sure, store-bought valentines are quick and easy, but just look at how gorgeous (and simple!) these handmade cards are. This sort of personal touch is incomparable!

SUNDAY	MONDAY	TUESDAY	WEDNESDAY	THURSDAY	FRIDAY	SATURDAY
November	2	hiking w/DAD 3	4	5	pickin' pumpkins 6	7
8	9	10	Veterans Day 11	12	13	Doug's B-Day 14
15	16	18	19	20	21	
22	23	St Louis Vacation 24	25	give thanks		28
first advent 29	30	NOVEMBER				

{ NOVEMBER }
by Tiffany Tillman

Set the mood.

I love how the rows of color on Tiffany's layout yield such a warm feeling. The look reminds me of an Impressionist painting.

Monthly Info:
Birthstones: Topaz, Citrine
Flower: Chrysanthemum
Astrological signs: Scorpio (Oct. 23–Nov. 21), Sagittarius (Nov. 22–Dec. 21)

FEBRUARY journaling and photography PROMPTS

DATE	JOURNALING JUMPSTARTS	PHOTO OPS
February 2: Groundhog Day	Do you want six more weeks of winter? Why or why not?	Something that's been revealed to you A realization you've made A secret
February 14: Valentine's Day	Who holds the key to your heart?	Heart shapes in clouds, flowers, etc.
February 24: National Tortilla Chip Day	What's your favorite snack?	Chips Salsa Snacks
Third Monday of February: Presidents' Day	Write about the most honest person you know.	Presidential statues at a local park
February: Mardi Gras	How do you celebrate your life?	A celebration Beaded necklaces
February: National Heart Month	How do you stay healthy?	Your family being active together Your exercise routine

NOVEMBER

GRATITUDE. November is for gratitude. It's the ideal time for cultivating family traditions—for getting together with loved ones, for enjoying the end of the fall season. November happens to be the month I became a U.S. citizen and has, hence, always been my favorite month. I'm so thankful for the life I'm privileged to lead!

"I WOULD **MAINTAIN** THAT THANKS ARE THE HIGHEST FORM OF **THOUGHT**, AND THAT **GRATITUDE** IS HAPPINESS DOUBLED **BY** WONDER."
—*Gilbert Keith Chesterton*

MARCH

GOOD FORTUNE. March is a transition month—it's about emerging from the doldrums of winter and looking forward to spring. Outside, the landscape is changing; the pace of life is quickening. Embrace the changes this year and relish the blessings all around you. Even if you aren't Irish, make green your color this month and look for everyday treasures.

"GUARD WELL YOUR SPARE **MOMENTS**. THEY ARE LIKE UNCUT **DIAMONDS**. DISCARD THEM AND THEIR VALUE WILL NEVER BE **KNOWN**. **IMPROVE** THEM AND THEY WILL BECOME THE BRIGHTEST **GEMS** IN A USEFUL LIFE."

—*Ralph Waldo Emerson*

OCTOBER **journaling** and **photography** PROMPTS

DATE	JOURNALING JUMPSTARTS	PHOTO OPS
October 9: Leif Eriksson Day	Write about something you've discovered in your life.	Beautiful things in your neighborhood Your best discoveries
Second Monday in October: Columbus Day	What's something you'd like to explore?	A park A museum
October 16: National Dictionary Day	Use the definition of a word in your journaling today.	A stack of dictionaries A trip to the library
October 16: National Boss Day	What's the best thing you've learned from a boss?	Your boss Your cubicle Your work "tools"
Fourth Sunday in October: Mother-in-Law's Day	Journal about your relationship with your mother-in-law.	Your mother-in-law Your husband
October 31: Halloween	What's your best childhood memory of Halloween?	Costumes Pumpkins Bowls full of Halloween candy

Daylight savings
starts
special night
Park day @1:30
Date night!
First day of spring
St. Patrick's Day
Zach's birthday
to the park...
no music class
get groceries
Joe's birthday
mar

MARCH
by Amanda Probst

Pick a color.

When in doubt, go monochromatic. Here, I focused on greens, selecting a few patterned pieces that coordinated and creating my calendar around them.

Monthly Info:
Birthstones: Aquamarine, Bloodstone
Flower: Jonquil
Astrological signs: Pisces (Feb. 19–Mar. 20), Aries (Mar. 21–Apr. 19)

{ MINI WREATH/
CANDLE BASE }

by Tracey Odachowski

Make your own leaf wreath.

I don't know about you, but I'm always on the lookout for ways to use my scrapbooking supplies in new ways. This mini-wreath centerpiece is a perfect example. Tracey created her own leaves with cardstock and watercolor pencils, and ended up with a totally customized piece for her home.

Like Valentine's, there wasn't much fanfare for St. Patrick's Day growing up. My mom, though, did pop green popcorn (still not sure how she did that) & serve green food on occasion. I definitely remember remembering to wear green &, in my younger days, trying to sneakily wear green so that others would think I wasn't & try to pinch me. I, then, of course, "got" to pinch them in turn & think highly of myself for being so cool.

Yeah. I was weird. I'm going to blame it on that green popcorn.

GREEN POPCORN
& PINCHING
by Amanda Probst

Let your text be your embellishment.

Call me odd, but this is one of my favorite layouts. I love how the word "green" just jumps out at you and how perfectly the stamp goes with the whole idea. Sometimes you just don't have the pictures you need to tell a story. In those cases, play around with your text. It can be just as visually interesting.

Once upon a time I was a little girl whose mom painstakingly crafted each of my Halloween costumes by hand. Unfortunately my little girl mind didn't appreciate her mother's efforts and couldn't see past the isles of Wonder Woman costumes and plastic masks. I grew up and soon came to realize how wrong I was. I quickly took on the role of costume seamstress. I started with a monkey costume for Grant when he was a year and half and I have been sewing

ever since. When I had Corinne the world of the princess opened its doors and swallowed us up. I waited 4 years for you to get big enough to fit this pattern and it came out beautiful so much better than I had envisioned. I know soon enough you will abandon your princess ways for something far cooler. My wish for you is that these costumes will stay in your memory forever and maybe someday you too will have a child who will enjoy a hand made Halloween. October 2004

HAPPY HALLOWEEN

hand made

halloween

fabric according to grain of pattern and fabric glory

{ HANDMADE HALLOWEEN }

by Summer Fullerton

Add a handmade touch.

Unlike me, Summer actually sews her kids' Halloween costumes. To document this tradition, she used actual remnants from a costume and photographs of the project-in-progress on her layout. I love the comfy feeling the fabric adds, but even more, I love that this layout is about making the costume, rather than the costume itself.

I suppose living in Colorado means I shouldn't be surprised that it sometimes (at least twice in the last four years) snows on Easter. When it does, it obviously calls for a revision of plans and expectations. Regardless, some aspects of Easter don't change. We always find time to dye eggs…the Easter Bunny still leaves goodies (though with 3 boys, those goodies are apt to be in a dump truck rather than a basket)… and we must have an egg hunt. The last couple years,

Some things never change...

we've made it to our neighborhood egg hunt as well, but we always hide eggs (empty plastic ones) in the backyard. Yes, even in the snow.

SOME THINGS NEVER CHANGE
by Amanda Probst

Use those "extra" photos.

We all have them: those "extra" photos from an event that somehow don't quite fit on your layout. Here are a couple of photos I took last Easter that just didn't go with the rest of my Easter pictures. I held on to them, though, and put them to use here to tell the story of our more general Easter traditions.

Give creative photo direction.

A surefire way to get great expressions from your kids is to let them "attack" you while you photograph them. Here, I challenged my son to "get me" with his pile of leaves and ended up with a fun series of photos. When I look at them, I feel like I really connected with him. I love how joy simply exudes from his face.

April 8, 2007

Argh! Ahoy, ye mateys! It's a pirate Easter!

The boys had recently taken an interest in everything pirate

TREASURE

so this year's Easter baskets were, um, pirate themed…complete with hats, bandanas,

hooks, daggers, short swords, eye patches and, obviously, the candy booty…

chocolate coins covered in gold and silver and copper. Noah took to being a pirate quickly and

easily, adopting the pirate stance and glare as if second nature.

Asher made for a rather endearing little pirate, capable of the glare but much quicker

to laugh. Micah, as was to be expected, was more interested in the candy than

Caribbean Sea

anything else (oh, and he got a bouncy ball instead of pirate hooks and daggers). But, Micah

won the Easter funny with his adorable swinging arm motion and "Argh!" cry every time we

asked what a pirate says. What fun…what treasure.

BlackBeard

{ TREASURE }
by Amanda Probst

Go themed!

Okay, I'll admit it. I deliberately planned a pirate-themed Easter so I could use some of these pirate-themed scrapbook supplies I had on hand. It helped that the boys thought it was all great fun, but truthfully, this is one of those layouts where I had the design and embellishments planned before I took the photos.

ALWAYS HAVE BEEN AND ALWAYS WILL BE SCARED OF ...

earths

eek

aliens

I'M NOT SURE WHY I FEAR THOSE FAKE, FULL-OF-ACID

ALIENS SIGOURNEY WEAVER ALIEN MOVIES. MAYBE IT'S THE

WAY THEY KILL ON SCREEN OR HOW THAT LITTLE ALIEN BABY

POPS OUT THE CHEST. EITHER WAY, I'M SCARED OF THOSE

MOVIES ... AND I'M NOT AFRAID TO ADMIT IT.

{ EARTH'S ALIENS }
by Tiffany Tillman

Admit your fears.

Halloween is the perfect time to document what scares you. When Tiffany presented this idea to me, I was so excited—why hadn't I thought of that! Now I have plans for layouts of my own to tell the stories of what I'm afraid of. Don't forget to ask your kids and significant other the same question!

them bad eggs...

I am usually not the one who purposely skips directions because I think I already know what to do. On the contrary, 99% of the time I read the directions fully, triple check that I have each little item necessary to accomplish the task and verify each step as I finish. But this wasn't one of those times. I pretty much figured egg dyeing (which you had begged so much to do) was idiot proof. I was wrong. I didn't realize I needed white vinegar to begin the process and didn't have bowls large enough to hold each egg AND the dye. We made a straight mess and the non stick glitter was the worst part. What was I thinking? Next year, I promise that I will read those little directions.

{ LOVE THEM BAD EGGS }
by Tiffany Tillman

Embrace your mistakes.

At first glance, this looks like just another egg-dyeing layout, right? Wrong! This layout is about neglecting to read the instructions and making a huge mess. I love that Tiffany turned it into a layout. I truly believe that it's moments like these we'll want to remember!

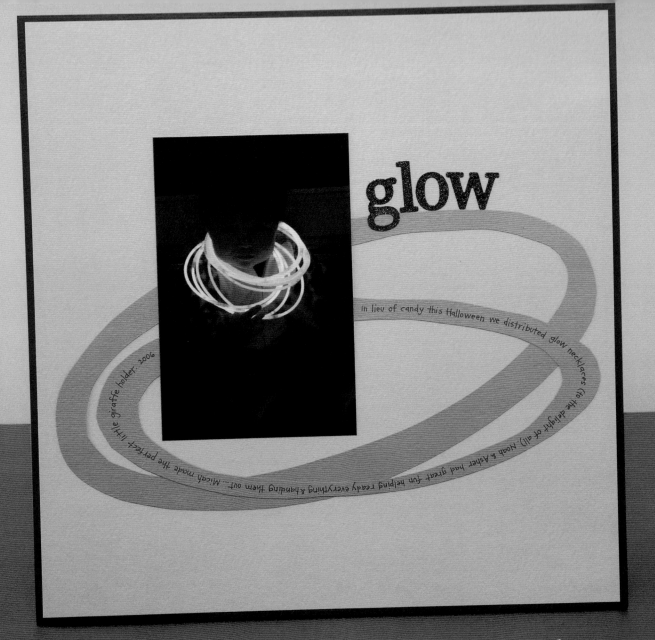

glow

In lieu of candy this Halloween we distributed glow necklaces (to the delight of all). Noah & Asher had great fun helping ready everything & handing them out... Micah made the perfect little giraffe holder. 2006

{ GLOW }
by Amanda Probst

Hand out something other than candy.

I wanted to mimic the glow necklaces we gave trick-or-treaters on this layout, I actually just free-handed these ovals. I sketched them in pencil on the reverse side of the cardstock and cut them out with scissors.

Life is good

Words simply aren't enough...sometimes I just sit & am amazed at how incredibly blessed I am...how very thankful. Pausing here to remember that...

{ LIFE IS GOOD }
by Amanda Probst

Make a layout just because.

I am incredibly fortunate. I know this. So, every now and then, I like to make a fun layout as a reminder of just how blessed—how happy—I am. Find something that makes you smile and create a quick layout to commemorate it.

many years of interesting and varied halloween costumes. minnie mouse of '83 is still my favorite.

83

Dig out old photos.

Laura managed to find photos of herself in 10 different Halloween costumes! I love seeing the progression and variety on this fun page. I managed to find a few pictures of myself in costumes, but I don't have one for every year. Thanks to their photo-loving mom, my boys definitely will!

COMP YOUTH ONE
COMP YOUTH ONE
COMP ADULT ONE
0.00

OREGON ZOO

REAL FUNNY.

This is the good stuff in life.

{REMEMBER}

Just add this to my list of things to be thankful for.

This morning we woke up, quickly dressed and hopped in the car to go to the zoo. I put the key in the ignition and turned – nothing happened the car was dead. Visions of our day going down the drain flashed through my mind. Roadside assistance came to our rescue. We were an hour off schedule and I could have just given up on the day; canceling our plans believing karma had planted a black cloud over us. But something quite unexpected happened instead. While waiting in line to get into the zoo a lady asked if we were members. When we responded no she handed us extra tickets and said she didn't want them to go to waste. All I could think was if we had arrived an hour earlier this wouldn't have happened. After a full day at the zoo we headed off to soccer practice. While Grant practiced 2 young men wheeled a cart into the park and set up an ice cream stand. The buzz quickly spread that they were giving away free ice cream and popsicles. Then if things couldn't have gotten any better a clown set up and put on a show for all the children. Was it luck or fate or simply karma teaching me a little lesson about not letting the little things in life get me down? Thank you karma I get it now. There's a lesson to be learned here.

LUCKY US

LUCKY US
by Summer Fullerton

Preserve your story as evidence.
Wow. Read the journaling here. Sometimes luck is just on your side. When it is, snap a few pictures and record the experience. You (and others) might not believe it later if you don't!

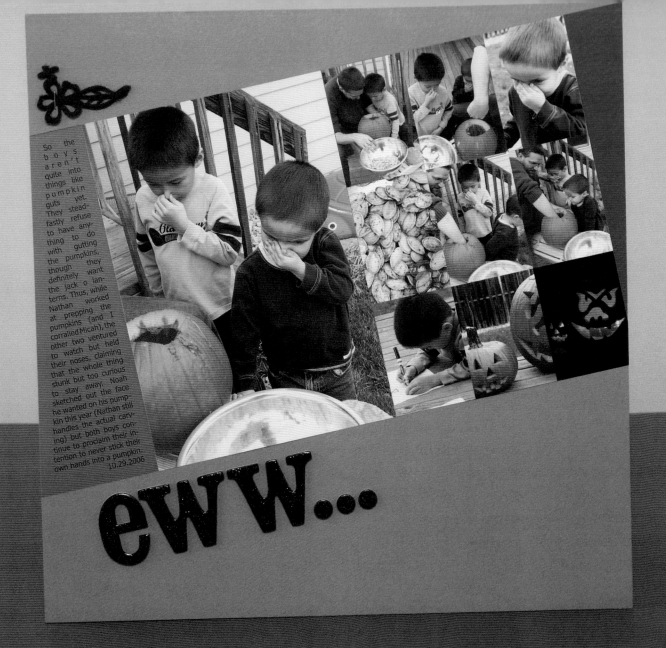

So the boys aren't quite into things like pumpkin guts yet. They steadfastly refuse to have anything to do with gutting the pumpkins, though they definitely want the jack o lanterns. Thus, while Nathan worked at prepping the pumpkins (and I corralled Micah), the other two ventured to watch but held their noses, claiming that the whole thing stunk but too curious to stay away. Noah sketched out the face he wanted on his pumpkin this year (Nathan still handles the actual carving) but both boys continue to proclaim their intention to never stick their own hands into a pumpkin. 10.29.2006

eww...

{ EWW . . . }
by Amanda Probst

Tilt things slightly.

One of my favorite ways to change up a very straight-forward layout is to simply tilt things just a bit. Here, I grouped my elements (dominant photo, supporting photos and journaling) but simply set things slightly askew to create more visual interest.

"Ah, springtime.
What a better way to
celebrate than going to
the park & discovering the
joys of making a "train"
to go down the tube slide.
The boys took turns
being the "engine" and even
though Micah was a
somewhat hesitant "caboose,"
it was all good fun.
March 18, 2007"

SLIDE INTO SPRINGTIME

by Amanda Probst

Keep your camera with you.

I have to admit, I don't always carry my camera with me. I just happened to have it this day and caught these delightful pictures of my boys having a blast together. This was the first time they'd tried going down the slide together, and I'd have missed it if I hadn't had my camera.

I'm not handy with a sewing machine. At all. So, I don't foresee any wonderful handmade costumes for my boys for Halloween. Fortunately, the local gently used stores have a great variety of ready-made costumes to choose from and the boys and I enjoy picking them out when fall starts. So far, it's a fine balancing act between buying "the" costume early enough that we can still find it in the right size and waiting long enough to make sure that the boys won't change their minds. I do my best to let the decision be theirs, and to date we've had fairly predictable choices. Nothing too original as of yet, but at least that means costumes are readily available, right? And just look at how cute they are!

October — Costumes

{ COSTUMES }
by Amanda Probst

Pick a single aspect of the holiday.

For this layout, I chose to focus on our family's tradition of trick-or-treating. I even went beyond trick-or-treating itself and documented the process behind picking costumes for trick-or-treating. Just as I'll want to remember what my boys dressed up as, I'll also want to remember why they chose those costumes.

LOVE YOU.

When I e-mailed mom and asked her to tell me more about this picture of her and her sister Lynn, here is what she said: "This was taken in my Uncle John Devine's back yard (sometime in the early 1950s). He was my grandfather's brother and had a gorgeous garden and always took great photos. This Kodachrome photo looks as good today as it did then....I still remember how special I felt in that outfit. It was gorgeous."

LOVE YOU
by Laura Kurz

Ask someone else to tell the story.
This is such a gorgeous old photo. But as with so many old photos that end up in our hands, Laura wasn't sure what was going on in the picture—what the story behind it was. To help, she e-mailed her mom and used the details she provided as her journaling.

My mom always made my costumes. They were utterly creative and never store-bought. I didn't appreciate the work and thought that went into that. Nor did I appreciate that my mom was one of those people who decorated for every holiday. For Halloween, there was always the bride of Dracula and a mummy hanging in the front windows…a witch on the front door…a scarecrow made of my dad's work clothes sitting on a bale of hay out front…corn stalks in bundles here and there. Now that I'm in charge of decorations and the like, it seems like a lot of work. I haven't really gotten into it yet, though I aspire to do so as the boys get older. I remember how the decorations, and more importantly the enthusiasm behind the decorations, set the stage for the season, making fall one of my favorites.

setting *the* **Stage**

geisha girl…pumpkin…mime…gypsy…clown…star…punk rocker

SETTING THE STAGE
by Amanda Probst

Visualize the past.

I began this page as a simple recollection of the Halloween costumes I wore growing up (notice the list on the right-hand side). As I was writing, though, I realized that what I remembered even more about celebrating Halloween as a child was how our home looked—the atmosphere my mom created. As it turns out, that was the important part.

Invite good fortune into your home.

To promote good fortune in your home, make this lovely framed accent (the Chinese symbol means "good fortune"). Have friends and family sign the glass with a dry-erase marker, or write weekly motivational messages to yourself.

october

			1	2	3 Railroad Museum free day	
4	5	6 Miller Farms field trip	7	8 library books due	9 co-op @ 1pm	10
11	12 Columbus Day	13 Circus in Denver?	14 park day @ 1:30 pm	15	16	17
18 Pumpkins @ the Farm	19 NCHA mtg @ 7pm	20 Zoo free day	21 JOHN	22 Special Night me & Asher	23	24
25	26	27	28	29 pick up candy	30	31 Halloween

Take a cue from nature.

To me, October is all about crisp, clear days, so I wanted a calendar with clean lines and simple graphics. Rather than sticking with more traditional fall colors, like reds, oranges and yellows, I selected just orange and added colors that complement it.

{ OCTOBER }
by Amanda Probst

Monthly Info:
Birthstones: Opal, Tourmaline
Flower: Calendula
Astrological signs: Libra (Sept. 23–Oct. 22),
Scorpio (Oct. 23–Nov. 21)

{ MARCH **journaling** and **photography** PROMPTS }

DATE	JOURNALING JUMPSTARTS	PHOTO OPS
March 2: Dr. Seuss's Birthday/ Read Across America Day	What's your favorite Dr. Seuss book?	A meal of "green eggs and ham" Your children reading at home or at the libary
March 11: Johnny Appleseed Day	Write about someone who has made a difference in your life.	A beautiful tree An orchard in bloom
March 17: St. Patrick's Day	How do you celebrate St. Patrick's Day?	Your favorite green items Green buds on trees
March: National Nutrition Month	What's your favorite healthy food?	Your favorite healthy dishes A stack of healthy cookbooks
March: National Women's History Month	If you were writing your own history, what would it say?	Influential women in your life
March 20: First Day of Spring	What represents spring to you?	The first flowers to peek through the soil Baby animals

OCTOBER

FALL. Fall is in full swing in October. Nature's beauty abounds and pumpkins are begging to be carved. But it won't be long before we feel the pull of the holidays. Just as the trees know when to change color in preparation for winter, start looking ahead to the holidays so you can pace yourself now!

"WINTER IS AN **ETCHING**, SPRING A **WATERCOLOR**, SUMMER AN OIL PAINTING AND AUTUMN A **MOSAIC** OF THEM ALL."

—*Stanley Horowitz*

{ APRIL }

{OCTOBER}

APRIL

SPRING. Ah, April. Flowers are in bloom, trees are adorned in green, rain cleanses the air. It's time for spring cleaning, wearing short-sleeved shirts and jumping in mud puddles. This month, celebrate the renewal of life and the return of warmth after a long winter. Celebrate spring!

"THE **STRONGEST** PRINCIPLE OF **GROWTH** LIES IN **HUMAN** CHOICE."

—*George Eliot*

SEPTEMBER **journaling** and **photography** PROMPTS

DATE	JOURNALING JUMPSTARTS	PHOTO OPS
September 1: Labor Day	How do you celebrate Labor Day?	Celebrations Relaxing at home Your workplace
First Sunday of September: Grandparents' Day	Journal about your relationship with your grandparents.	Your grandparents Interactions between your children and their grandparents
September 11: Patriot Day	Where were you on 9/11 and how has it affected your life?	Flags Memorial ceremonies
September 17: Constitution Day	If you were going to write your own constitution, what would it say?	Your state capital building Symbols of freedom
September 22: First Day of Fall	What symbolizes fall for you?	Changing leaves Crisp red apples Your fall traditions
September: Back to School	Describe your favorite classes and most influential teachers.	The school bus School supplies Your child's classroom

april

		April Fool's Day			
		1	2	3	4
neighborhood egg hunt			special Night: me & Noah	co-op @ 1:00 pm	
5	6	7	8	9	10	11
Easter			taxes due			
12	13	14	15	16	17	18
	Bekah's birthday NCHA mtg 7pm		Earth Day			
19	20	21	22	23	24	25
				free day at zoo		
26	27	28	29	30		

wonder

adventure

discover

{ APRIL }
by Amanda Probst

Dig out your vellum.

Remember vellum? Doesn't it just scream "spring" to you? I love how the vellum calendar softens the photos behind it; it allowed me to keep the color and detail without sacrificing utility.

Monthly Info:
Birthstone: Diamond
Flowers: Sweet Pea, Daisy
Astrological signs: Aries (Mar. 21–Apr. 19), Taurus (Apr. 20–May 20)

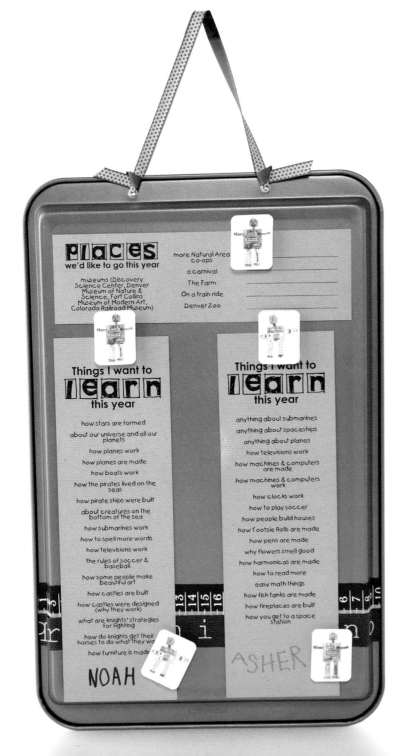

by Amanda Probst

Ask your kids.

This is something I started doing last year: asking my kids what it was they wanted to learn in the coming school year. It's informative and quite fun! To make it a bit more "official" this year, we typed up the lists. I mounted them on a cookie sheet turned magnetic display board and added Shrinky-Dink artwork the boys had drawn as magnets.

Spring. Growing up, spring meant smudge season and picking up the pace from our leisurely winters as we readied ourselves for summer. For those who don't know, smudge season is a way of life if you live on an orchard. My dad's whole schedule would change as he'd be called upon to wake in the middle of the night to go light the smudge pots to try to keep the trees warm and prevent a frost once fruit had begun to develop. He had all these gadgets to tell him when it dropped below a certain temperature in different parts of the orchard. He pretty much went to bed right after dinner and was up at night and then again at sunrise as normal to start the day. So smudge season signaled the time of year when we'd start seeing less and less of my dad. He would be busy tending the orchards and readying everything for the harvests. His being "on call" meant that we never ventured far from home during the spring. We understood. But, is it any wonder that spring is my least favorite season?

smudge season

{ SMUDGE SEASON }
by Amanda Probst
photos by Cassandra Smith

Keep it simple.

I didn't really realize how I felt about spring until I started writing this story down. I knew it was something I wanted to document, because it was such a big part of the rhythm of our years growing up. Lacking any photos, I sent my sister out to take some for me, picked my favorite and added a simple title to create my page.

just one glance

Sometimes some photos make me laugh & cry with just one glance. This picture is 10 years old taken the day I graduated from high school. The woman I'm proudly standing next to with diploma in hand is my Grandma who passed earlier this year. I miss her; it makes me cry. Other times I peek at this photo and laugh because I thought I knew it all then. Come to find out, I didn't know so much and I've spent the last 10 years learning just how much I really didn't and still don't know. In this one photo, I'm reminded to never stop learning or growing and more importantly to cherish my family every single day. There is a power in this picture that only takes a glance for me to see.

{ JUST ONE GLANCE }
by Tiffany Tillman

Write what a photo makes you feel.

Tiffany did an excellent job with her journaling. She lays it out there and explains what she feels when she sees this particular photo. Some photos are like that—they're the ones worth more than a thousand words. Find a photo that tells an entire story all by itself, then write that story down.

It wasn't a conscious decision, but we've found that since living in Colorado the start of spring means taking the boys to the park to feed the geese. Not that we hadn't been to the park all winter, but there always seemed to be a day in mid-March where Nathan and I would spontaneously decide to make an outing of it as a family, stopping for lunch and taking goldfish crackers for the geese before playing at the park. Just a special afternoon altogether, enjoying the warming weather and the growth all around us. We'd never noted the date before. Looking back through our pictures, though, it's definitely a trend. Now that we recognize it, we hope to make it an annual event. I love the idea of "officially" celebrating the start of spring as a family.

{ START OF SPRING }
by Amanda Probst

Start a tradition.

Until I started thinking about what we do during the spring, I didn't recognize that we'd already started a routine of sorts. Now that I see it, this park outing is sure to become a "start of spring" tradition.

I suppose I've always been what some would call "artistic." I've definitely always had an interest in it. In my preteen years, I remember taking oil and acrylic painting classes with my mom. We'd go at night along with our neighbor and her daughter (my best friend at the time). My mom still has some of those works hanging in the house. In high school, I ran out of art class options and ended up creating my own. In college, I somehow decided not to major in art or anything related, but managed to take a number of art classes as my personal release from academia. I even landed a job in the publications department. Then I graduated and got married and went to law school. And my art classes went on hiatus. After Noah was born, though, Nathan and I decided that we each needed some creative outlet in our lives and started by signing up for art classes through the city parks and rec department. Nathan took stained glass (I couldn't due to the lead since I was still nursing), and I took watercolor painting. It was like coming home…gathering the supplies and using them to CREATE. That's what art classes are all about. Since those classes in Eugene, I've not taken any more art classes. Scrapbooking has become my outlet instead. But. Now that I'm thinking about it and the boys are a bit older, I might just look into the art class offerings around here…dust off those watercolor brushes and paints or maybe tackle a new medium altogether. For me, it's not so much about learning some new technique (though that's always fun). It's about a set time to focus on creativity one on one, just you and your art. How cool is that.

Document your favorite creative tools.

{ ART CLASS }
by Amanda Probst

It's easy to neglect the tools of the trade in your hobbies. I've made layouts about why I love scrapbooking and about creativity in general, but I haven't stopped and taken the time to actually document what I use when I create. Here, I focused on the watercolor painting supplies I've acquired over the years through a number of just-for-me classes I've enjoyed.

Yes, Noah & Asher are still in pjs. Yes, that's the middle of the street (our fortunately very quiet street). Yes, they're playing in the puddle. It's like this. It rained that morning. The mobile AC guy was there working on our van in the garage. The boys, ever curious, insisted on being outside so they could see what he was doing. While outside, they discovered the aforementioned puddle. Asher started it by heading out on his trike. Micah was quick to follow, with Noah pushing so Micah need not get his feet wet. Noah was soon leaping & splashing & encouraging his brothers to do the same. At this point, Asher retreated for the dry house. Micah, still hesitant, stood by the edge & cheered Noah on before finally stomping through the puddle on his own. I'm sure the AC guy thought I was odd. After all, rather than calling them out of the street or anything else, I ran inside to get my camera & asked them to splash some more. That's what puddles are for, right?

what Puddles R for...

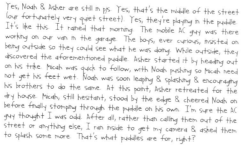

{ WHAT PUDDLES R FOR }

by Amanda Probst

Play in the street.

I'm not sure my kids realize how they benefit from me being the scrapbooking mom I am. Instead of telling them to get out of the street and stop making a mess in the puddle, I grabbed a camera and directed them to do it some more!

are you there god?
it's me Margaret

babysitter's club

just as long as
we're together

my brother sam
is dead

how to eat
fried worms

summer of my
german soldier

what jamie saw

i have always loved to read
even as a young girl,
i would stay up well past
my bedtime to finish
just one more chapter
these were just a few of
my favorites from
the fourth grade.

where the
red fern grows

tales of a fourth
grade nothing

{ LOVE TO READ }
by Laura Kurz

Remember your favorite school subject.

What was your favorite subject growing up? Laura found this picture of herself from around fourth grade, reading, as usual. On her layout, she wrote about her love of reading and listed some of the books she read at that age. Even if you can't find pictures of yourself enjoying your favorite subject, take pictures of books or equipment that relates to it.

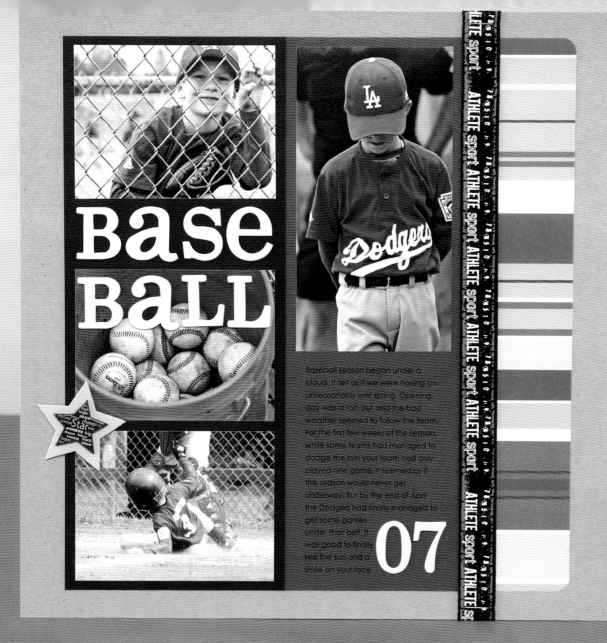

BASE BALL

Baseball season began under a cloud. It felt as if we were having an unseasonably wet spring. Opening day was a rain out and the bad weather seemed to follow the team. For the first few weeks of the season, while some teams had managed to dodge the rain your team had only played one game. It seemed as if the season would never get underway. But by the end of April the Dodgers had finally managed to get some games under their belt. It was good to finally see the sun and a smile on your face.

07

{ BASEBALL
by Summer Fullerton }

Add some green.

Red, blue and green is one of my all-time favorite color combinations. On this layout, I love how Summer didn't stick with just the colors of her son's jersey, but added some green. It just brings the whole thing to life, don't you think? Green goes so well with all of spring—the new leaves, the new growth. So I say, when in doubt, add green!

We do a lot of our "big" talks in the car. This was no exception. I don't remember exactly when it was (I want to say spring of 2004). I do remember, though, driving along this road north of Fort Collins...admiring the scenery and discussing our reasons for wanting to homeschool. More importantly, we were listing what we wanted for our children. I compiled that list and made out this mission statement of sorts, with the intention of framing it to hang in our home as a reminder. I've yet to do that, though I've carried it with me in my calendar routinely. Regardless, we *have* adopted homeschooling into our lives and the plan is to continue doing so. This mission statement still holds true today and will, I think, help guide us into the future.

By choosing to homeschool, we hope to...

• Foster a lifetime love of learning

• Provide the tools and atmosphere to encourage our children to think critically

• Cultivate loving, helpful and healthy relationships between our sons and ourselves

• Enable our children to obtain information they require (through knowing how to read well and knowing where and how to find needed information)

• Enable our children to communicate effectively with others both orally and in writing

• Provide a broad general knowledge base from which our children can draw as needed

• Instill the math knowledge required for daily life, as well as an awareness, if not a working knowledge, of how higher math shapes the world

• Encourage qualities of self-confidence and responsibility in our children for their choices and their actions

• Promote a sense of respect for the community and an attitude of service

• Enjoy and cherish the time we have with our children...learning alongside them

{ THE ROAD AHEAD }
by Amanda Probst

Write a mission statement.

This is one of those layouts where the journaling came first. Because the words are so essential, I didn't want to take the focus away from them with a distracting photo or a number of embellishments. Rather, I added a single photo that ties in nicely with the story. Simple, but the words are what's important here.

Our experience raising
Painted Lady butterflies...

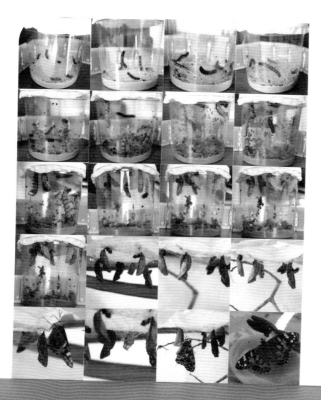

metamorphosis

The boys loved watching
our caterpillars turn into
butterflies, but were sad to
see them go.
We released them in the
front yard and set out
marigolds,
hoping they'll
come back to visit.

{ METAMORPHOSIS }
by Amanda Probst

Raise some butterflies.

If you haven't tried raising butterflies at home, consider it. We sent off for these kits along with the rest of our home-school group and had so much fun watching our little caterpillars grow. In just three weeks, we had beautiful butterflies as well as a concrete lesson in the wonders of spring and life cycles.

BACKPACKS LOADED
LUNCHES PACKED
EXCITEMENT
FILLS THE AIR
IT IS THE 1ST
DAY OF SCHOOL

SCHOOL
SPEED
LIMIT
20
SCHOOL DAYS
7AM-5PM

4TH GRADE

SEPTEMBER
6th

1ST GRADE

b A+ ck {2} SCHOOL
student

Take "first day" photos.

This is one of my favorite layouts by Summer. I love the wonderful colors and that fabulous tall photo down the side of the page. Even though the pictures are all of the same day, the different color treatments and blocks of patterns create a lively layout.

I know that this is not a pretty picture, but this whole spring cleaning business is something new for us. We're more used to 'Spring Moving.' Suddenly, however, we realized this spring that we desperately needed to go through the garage, closets, playroom, and whatever else and do a major purge. We have grown so accustomed to having to do this every time we were unpacking from our many moves that it never occurred to us we would have to do it on a regular basis when we finally managed to stay put somewhere. So much needs to go. Our baby days have come to an end, and with them, so has the need for high chairs, car seats, and all of those little baby toys and clothes. Our bedroom underwent a cosmetic overhaul, so out go the old linens and decorations. There are dishes and appliances in the kitchen that simply don't get used, so out they go as well. From the sounds of it, a profitable garage sale just might be in our future!

{ SPRING CLEANING }
by Tracey Odachowski

Accept the inevitable.

Spring cleaning is just a part of life. Rather than sweep it under the rug (along with who knows what else), welcome it into your life as the opportunity it is. Personally, I enjoy spring cleaning and find excuses to do it throughout the year.

field trip

for some fabulous field trips. This one, our first, was at the Pineridge Natural Area and covered different bird beaks as tools. We then went on a bird watching walk. The boys loved using the binoculars and spotting many signs of bird life for their scavenger hunts. Ash made a new friend who helped him out while I chased Micah...a fun day.

Our homeschool group co-op teamed up with the city's Master Naturalist program volunteers

{ FIELD TRIP }
by Amanda Probst

Go on a field trip.

Accompanying your child on a field trip provides awesome photo opportunities. On this particular trip, I was fortunate to have an extra pair of hands to assist two of my boys while I chased down my youngest, who was drawn to the water and high grasses.

So we were in the backyard just hanging out. I had the camera out for some reason. Suddenly, Noah was inspired and declared that we had to play a new game...Photo Tag! Intrigued and obviously sensing a good photo op, I asked how one plays Photo Tag. He explained that I simply had to try to take their picture while they ran wildly around the yard. Once I caught them X number of times (amazingly this number kept going up), I'd win. And off they went. What a wonderful new game...it really was great fun trying to catch them as they ducked behind things and even tried hiding inside the sandbox. In the end, I think everybody won, as we were all laughing and having a blast. 4.20.07

Photo
tag

y z a

A FUN NEW GAME—
JUST CLICK AND TRY TO
CATCH THE BOYS IN
THE FRAME...

u v w

{ PHOTO TAG }
by Amanda Probst

Make photography a game.

Every now and again, forget about things like focus and composition and just have fun with your camera. On this particular afternoon, the boys decided we should play "photo tag," which consisted of me trying to capture them on film while they sprinted to and fro around the yard. Obviously the photos aren't perfect, but look at the great energy and movement. You can just feel the joy!

We don't do official back to school shopping these days... no new pencils or paper or clothes. Since we homeschool, there's really no need. Yet, I can't seem to stop myself when September rolls around. It seems to be ingrained in me...to be drawn to all the curricula available. I love to browse through the educational and homeschool catalogs and the shelves at the bookstores, looking for the perfect books to add to our collection.

i ♥ books

{ I LOVE BOOKS }
by Amanda Probst

Share your love of knowledge.

We've all seen layouts about our favorite drinks and favorite places and even our favorite colors, but here, I wanted to record my general love of books, especially educational books. I considered having the layout focus on my sons using these books but decided that the books themselves tell the story.

march 2007

favorite signs of
SPRING

Spring is much more enjoyable in Virginia than in Texas. For one, it lasts a lot longer and distinctively makes you feel refreshed after a long, gray winter. Two of the most noticeable plants bloom too. I call them 'the best scent' and 'the worst scent'. One (the pink one) smells as a flower should: fresh and sweet. The other smells like rubber; no joke! My favorite part is finally resuming our mid-morning walk around the neighborhood. It's too early to go without jackets but it's still beautiful.

{ SIGNS OF SPRING }
by Tiffany Tillman

Photograph your favorites.

With the change of seasons, don't forget to stop and photograph some of your favorite things. Here, Tiffany captured three of her favorite signs of spring. The added journaling brings the photos to life—I actually want to smell the flower that smells like rubber!

going back

Back to school. How I've always loved those three little words. Yes, I was one of *those* people. The people who looked forward to school starting again...who was maybe more excited by shopping for school supplies than shopping for back to school clothes (though it was close!)...who busily checked and re-checked to make sure everything was in order before that first day. As the start of school neared, I remember the annual debate with myself over whether to try to get into the school year schedule ahead of time (waking up earlier and going to bed sooner) or stretch out my late nights until the last possible day. (The late nights won.) I remember, also, a recurring dream almost every year the night before the first day. Unlike some who might be apprehensive about school and dream of embarrassing moments in front of classmates, I dreamt of oversleeping and missing the bus...running after it as it drove off, only to wake up and discover that it was just a dream. I could then be relieved and get ready for school. I was usually one of the first ones up (after my dad) and was in charge of getting everyone else up and going. We caught the bus in front of our house. In the mornings, we would wait out front, maybe grabbing an apple off a nearby tree if it was the right season. We were toward the end of the morning route, so were only on the bus 15-20 minutes before reaching school. In the afternoons, though, we were toward the end of the route and sometimes were on the bus for as much as an hour. I don't remember ever minding this much, as it gave me time to get some homework done or other things. Yup, I loved going back to school.

Zach & me waiting for the bus 1990

{ GOING BACK }
by Amanda Probst

Record your enthusiasm.

I can't help it. I love back-to-school time. Even though I'm not the one going back to school, the start of September brings memories of excitement and happiness that I wanted to document on this layout.

My surprise flower of the year. Comes in a variety of colors and can withstand shade, sun, and full sun. Really resilient, have in most of my pots this year. Will definitely use again next year, maybe even in beds in backyard that get full sun. Had two versions - white with pink center and white with yellow center. Purchased in early/late May/early June.

vinca

GARDEN JOURNAL

by Laura Kurz

Create a reference.

You probably aren't as obsessive as I am and don't hold onto all of the packaging that comes with flowers, plants and seeds. While I usually toss them all into a drawer, Laura, brilliant woman that she is, created this handy little book to keep notes about her garden to reference in coming years. She plans to make more pages as she goes. Wonderful!

07

garden journal

September

Sun	Mon	Tues	Wed	Thurs	Fri	Sat
		1 *Emily's B-Day*	2	3	4	5
6	7 *Labor Day*	8	9	10	11 *Patriot Day*	12
13 *Grandparent's Day*	14	15	16	17 *Constitution Day*	18	19 *Rosh Hashanah*
20	21	22 *1st Day of Fall*	23	24	25	26
27 *Gabe's B-Day*	28 *Yom Kippur*	29	30			*Back to School*

{ SEPTEMBER }
by Tracey Odachowski

Think back to school.

From the ruler markings to the notebook paper, Tracey took the back-to-school theme seriously with her September calendar page. It makes me want to practice my penmanship!

Monthly Info:
Birthstone: Sapphire
Flower: Aster
Astrological signs: Virgo (Aug. 23–Sept. 22), Libra (Sept. 23–Oct. 22)

APRIL **journaling** and **photography** PROMPTS

DATE	JOURNALING JUMPSTARTS	PHOTO OPS
April 1: April Fools' Day	Do you play practical jokes on people? What are some of your favorites?	Fun practical jokes, both the planning and the execution Your family or children giggling about something silly
April 2: International Children's Book Day	Who is your favorite fairytale character and why?	Children reading Your favorite bookstore A shelf full of books
April 15: Income Taxes Due	Do you wait until the last minute, or do you file your taxes in January?	Dropping your taxes in the mail The line of people at the post office on tax day
April 22: Earth Day	How does the theme of "reduce, reuse, recycle" play out in your life?	Your recycling efforts Things you do to help the environment
April: Spring Break	How do you celebrate spring break? How did you celebrate it in the past?	Fun things you do during spring break A road trip
April: Easter	What are your family Easter traditions?	Easter baskets Dyed eggs, bunnies, baby animals (Visit a petting zoo!)

SEPTEMBER

EDUCATION. It happens every year: we stock up on school supplies and new clothes in preparation for another school year. That's why September is about education—not only for our children but for ourselves. September means getting back into the swing of things after a slow-paced summer. It offers us a wonderful opportunity to grow by taking a community class or even just checking out a good book at the library. As you send the kids off to school (or simply watch others do so), think about something you'd like to learn, then take steps to make it happen.

"I AM STILL LEARNING."

—Michelangelo

{SEPTEMBER}

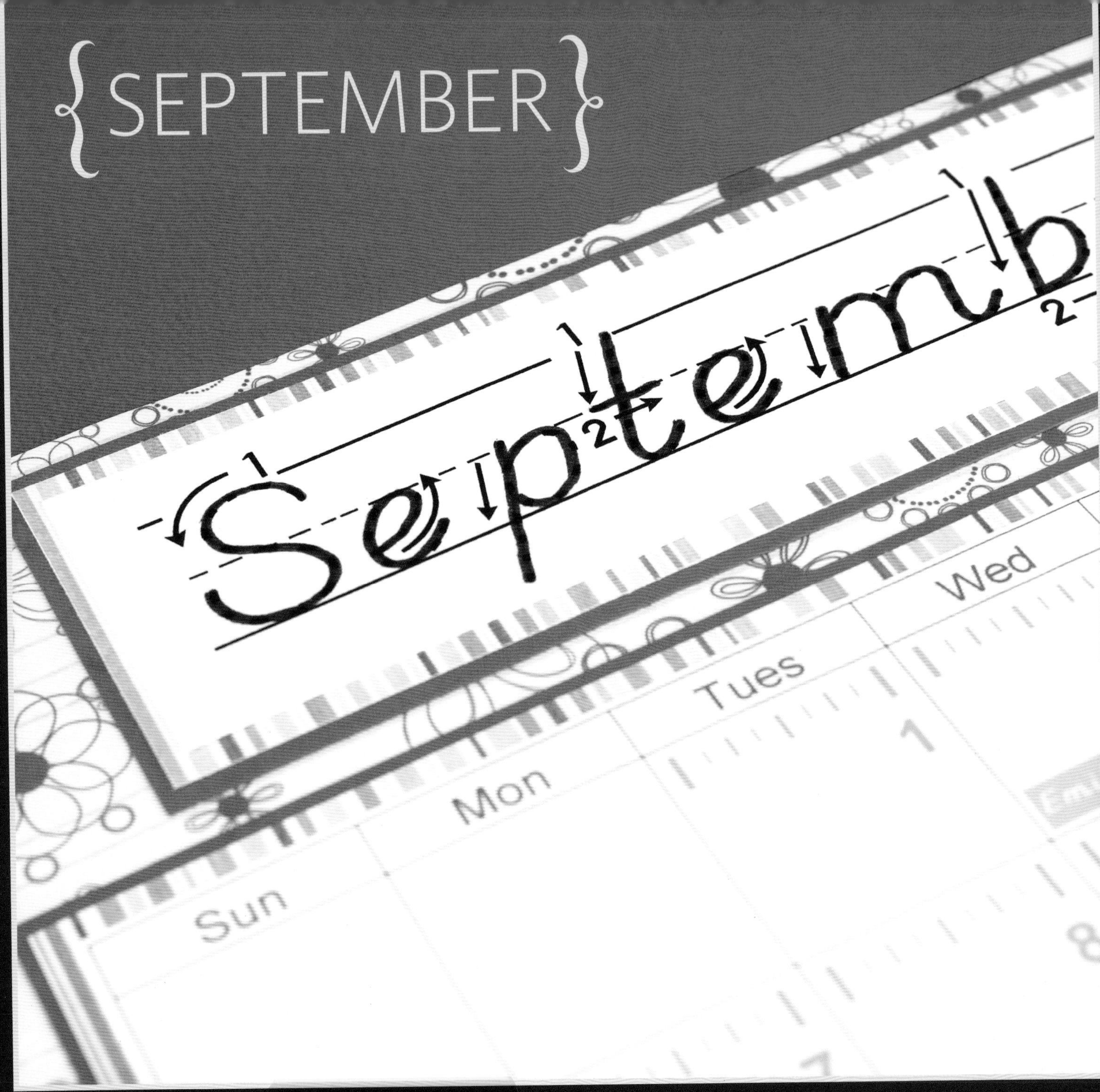

MAY

APPRECIATION. With Mother's Day and Memorial Day this month, May is dedicated to appreciating those who have touched your life. Take some time to reflect on your relationship with your mom or another special woman in your life. Consider those who came before you and those who will come after. Think about the cycle of life and your place in it. Growing up, May was always crazy-busy in our house, with end-of-the-school-year stuff and the cherry harvest not far away. Taking time to celebrate these special holidays provided a moment for us to stop and be grateful.

"BEING **DEEPLY** LOVED BY SOMEONE GIVES YOU STRENGTH; **LOVING** SOMEONE **DEEPLY GIVES** YOU COURAGE."
—*Lao Tzu*

AUGUST **journaling** and **photography** PROMPTS

DATE	JOURNALING JUMPSTARTS	PHOTO OPS
First Sunday of August: Friendship Day	Jot down the reasons why you love your friends.	A date with a friend for lunch, shopping or scrapbooking Candid shots of your friends
August 13: International Lefthander's Day	Celebrate the left-handed people in your life.	Shots of you using your left hand (or right hand) for a day Photos of left-handed friends and family members
August 19: National Aviation Day	National Aviation Day celebrates the dawn of aviation and the beginning of airline flights. Journal about your first flight on an airplane.	A local air show A flight museum Airplanes
August 26: National Women's Equality Day	What would your life be like if women didn't have the right to vote?	Election signs Campaign buttons
August: Family Vacations	What are your travel traditions now? What were they like as a child?	Maps Suitcases Modes of transportation (planes, trains, boats)
August: Summer Sports	What sports do you and your family enjoy in the summer?	Baseball games Fans in the bleachers Sports equipment

may

{ MAY }
by Amanda Probst

Use your scraps.

One of my very favorite things is using up my scraps. It gives me a strangely satisfying feeling of accomplishment. Simply find some scrap pieces of patterned paper (they don't even have to coordinate if you don't want them to), cut them to the same size and arrange them in a calendar format. Add a few embellishments and stamps, and you're good to go!

Monthly Info:
Birthstone: Emerald
Flowers: Lily of the Valley, Hawthorne
Astrological signs: Taurus (Apr. 20–May 20), Gemini (May 21–June 20)

{ TRAVEL TOTE }

by Summer Fullerton

Take it with you.

Summer made this great tote for use when traveling. She printed used digital brushes on iron-on transfer material for the brown floral design and sewed on clear vinyl to make a pocket for sundries. I also love that she removed the original handles on the canvas tote and made her own with ribbon!

Most of my holiday memories center around lots of family and great food (I really miss that food), but Memorial Day is a little different. My memories of Memorial Day weekend are of beautiful sunny days gathering flowers from our yard (pink peonies by the bucket-full, literally). My dad would gather jars and cans and wrap them in tin foil (I'm still not sure why he did that). Then he'd put some large rocks in the bottom for weight. We'd take all this to the local cemetery, where we'd add water and flowers to the jars to make little arrangements. Next, we'd scout out the graves of my dad's parents, aunts, uncles, cousins and various other relatives and leave a jar or two at each spot. Usually my dad and I would stop and say a little prayer silently while standing at my grandpa's grave. He died when I was five, so none of my siblings really ever knew him. I don't have clear memories but do, at least, have some pictures and remember the feelings that surrounded my grandpa…warmth and laughter and goodness. Since he was (at the time) the only relative who'd died that I'd actually known in life, setting flowers at his grave was always more special to me. Growing up, I held him secretly in my heart as a kind of guardian angel. So…I miss visiting the cemetery with my parents. I know, though, that returning to Prosser every Memorial Day isn't practical right now and that it wouldn't mean the same to my boys. Regardless, I'd like to share that with them at least once…to tell them the stories of their ancestors and show them this part of where they came from.

MEMORIAL DAYS

by Amanda Probst
photos by Cassandra Smith

Respect the past.

Cemeteries may seem like dreary places to many, but they were always a very peaceful part of my childhood. I felt so connected to family history while we were there. On this layout, I wanted to share that feeling with my own sons, even though they've never been to this particular cemetery.

when i lived in london

we started planning a long-weekend trip

to paris almost immediately.

and i had this really, really annoying mental block.

i kept calling the eiffel tower the empire state building.

don't ask me why. i'm not from new york.

the two structures look nothing alike.

the only thing they share is the "e"

well, for the past week i've been telling people

we're going to scotland in september.

we're not going to scotland.

we're going to ireland.

so today, i go to get my passport picture and

the lady is being nice and asks where we are traveling.

"scotland," i said, without a second thought.

ugh.

{ SCOTLAND }

by Laura Kurz

Laugh at yourself.

Laura used this simple passport photo to tell the story of how she keeps getting confused and telling people she's going to Scotland for an upcoming vacation (she's really going to Ireland and England). Personally, I'm impressed at how great her passport photo looks!

may

Once a mom, always a mom. It's one of those rare titles that never expires. It may have additions over the years ... may become "Nana" after awhile. But it'll still always be MOM. Here's mine. My mom that is. Need to take more pictures of the two of us together!

always mOm

{ ALWAYS MOM }
by Amanda Probst

Pose with your mom.

When my mom came to visit last May, I suddenly realized I couldn't remember the last time we'd had a picture taken together. Don't let those moments when you're together pass without documenting them.

Long summer days...playing in the front yard. The boys have always loved "chasing" their shadows and lately have taken to making shadow puppets on walls. Asher was delighted to learn that the driveway makes for one big wall and set about trying out all sorts of poses.

shadow play

{ SHADOW PLAY }
by Amanda Probst

Play in your own backyard.

Summer days are the perfect opportunity for playing with your shadow. When I caught Asher posing in the driveway, I had to grab the camera, envisioning a layout about the "long" days of summer.

I am constantly amazed at how entertaining simple sidewalk chalk can be. It's a beautiful thing...to watch Micah learn the joys of it by observing his brothers...to see Asher grow more confident in his writing and drawing abilities...to witness Noah's introduction of water to the situation and the resulting delight. What a perfect spring afternoon activity! According to Noah, it was...

chalk-o-rif-fic!

(Yes, he really said that. When I jokingly asked him how to spell it, he said, "Just take a 'riffic' and add it to 'chalk.'" Of course.)

{ CHALK-O-RIF-FIC }
by Amanda Probst

Play with chalk.

Is there anything better than sidewalk chalk? Well, there's always sidewalk chalk plus water. These photos were taken on a day I'd deliberately set aside to just enjoy with my boys. I'd been away and then sick and wanted to spend some quality time with them. This is what they wanted to do, and I couldn't have been happier!

spot spot spot

Most people who know my Dad know that he's a nut. He's a goofball, a person that loves to belly laugh and crack a few jokes to get others to laugh too. I don't know him as anything else matter of fact. So, I wasn't too surprised when he and Mom shared this photo of him on some rock next to a large beach in the Caribbean. Dad was made to enjoy life. But looking at the picture made me think of something else: I've never been outside the U.S. and at some point I would love to visit the Caribbean, or Australia or Europe, or anything -- it's all good, and enjoy my vacation spot. Even if at the end of my vacation I look back and realize the ONLY photo I took of myself was on ... "some rock".

{ SPOT
by Tiffany Tillman }

Live vicariously through others.
I love this story about Tiffany's dad on vacation. Even more, I love how she added journaling about her own vacation dreams.

{ CROP GALS }
by Tracey Odachowski

Celebrate friends.

Tracey, lucky gal that she is, gets together with these fabulous women at least once a month to scrapbook. In honor of National Scrapbook Day, she created this layout to celebrate their friendship. The journaling is cleverly hidden beneath the bottom-right.

hometown adventure

Lacking the time and resources to take a "real" vacation but in need of a break, we decided to spend a day being tourists in our own hometown. The boys kept asking where we were going and all we would tell them was that we were going on a "mysterious adventure" which, of course, was not a satisfactory answer. We headed to the visitor center, posed as tourists, and asked the helpful staff there what they would recommend seeing given just one afternoon. Following their advice, we went next to the Swetsville metal sculpture park where the boys marveled at all of the metal animals and make believe vehicles and made music at the giant wind chime looking thing. Then we headed up to Old Town (always a favorite) for some ice cream and fountain play, stopping to browse in a gallery along the way. The fountain play was spectacular fun with three standing sculptures that squirted jets of water from one base to the next to the next with perfect aim. We took a LOT of pictures. Aside from the ice cream, these were all things we hadn't done as a family before. Just think of all the other cool things our own town has to offer that we haven't experienced yet...

{ HOMETOWN ADVENTURE }
by Amanda Probst

Tour your own hometown.

I'm pretty proud of this one. What began as a fun idea to play tourist in our own hometown turned into a day jam-packed with sheer delight—and 432 pictures. A friend challenged me to use all of them on one layout. I think I rose to the occasion! I love having them all here (okay, I left out 23), and we truly enjoyed getting to know our own town better.

My sweet Noah has been
picking flowers for me lately.
It's a perk of motherhood.
Others include: sincere smiles in
gratitude for the simplest things...
warm baby hugs first thing in the
morning...having your children
believe that you know everything
and have magic...getting to
say "because I'm the Mommy.

for me?

that's why"...watching your
child's personality develop...
the opportunity to see the
world's wonders through
a child's eyes...being able
to heal an injury with
just a kiss...snuggling in
the afternoon with a good
book...the spark in your
child's eyes when he learns
something new thanks to
you...growing eyes in the back
of your head...the complete
awe when those babes are
first placed in your arms...being
the keeper of your children's
milestones and memories...

{ FOR ME? }
by Amanda Probst

List the perks of motherhood.

Last May, my boys started bringing me flowers on a regular basis. As I sincerely thanked them each and every time, I started thinking about the benefits of being a mom and decided to list some of them. This layout is the result. What do you think the perks of motherhood are?

HerSHEY

August 16, 2006

Just a few photos from our second trip to Hersheypark. Emily is now at "Twizzler" height, & Gabe is just barely still a "Reece's Peanut Butter Cup." A new thing for us was the monorail ride around the park, catching the views from above. The smell of chocolate remains the same!

{ HERSHEY }
by Tracy Odachowski

Include the side trips.

For several years in a row, Tracey's summer family trip was to Hershey, Pennsylvania. Of course, this included a side trip to Hershey Park for the day. Her kids still consider it one of their favorite places to go. And I have to thank Tracey for enlightening me; I've now added Hershey to my list of places to visit!

Don't tell my boss,
but I actually **LIKE** going to work

I like the kids, I like the WORK
And I even like the cafeteria food.

St. Paul's has been
A breath of **FRESH** air.

A place that embraces new **IDEAS**
And that gives credit where it's due.

While understanding the importance of balancing
Your life and YOUR work.

It makes me want to be a better employee —
To always **TRY** harder.

Now, that's refreshing.

{ DON'T TELL
MY BOSS }
by Laura Kurz

Appreciate your job.

Laura works at this school and loves it. This page is all about how she appreciates that work and the perspective it gives her. Everyone should be so fortunate. What about you? What do you value about your job?

We hadn't been camping in ages. When a friend offered the use of his cabin for the weekend, we jumped at the opportunity and hurriedly planned an impromptu camping trip. Some of the highlights:

getting new sleeping bags for the boys (why didn't they make them like this years ago?)

trying to remember how to pack for camping (and realizing that packing for camping with three young boys is an entirely different thing)

games by candlelight (the electricity and running water we'd planned on were out of commission upon arrival...which made things a little bit trickier but still fun...and offered an opportunity for a mini history lesson on life before electricity after moving all oil lamps out of Micah's reach)

s'mores by the campfire, though Noah and Asher were not impressed (weirdos)

cozy fireplace inside the cabin, where Micah and I slept in the guest room (Nathan & the other boys opted to sleep in the tent)

yummy breakfast over a gas grill

taking an "exploring walk" (Asher refused to take a "hike") that was maybe a mile round trip, what with short legs and all

Noah and I holding things up as we continually stopped to take pictures

a little climb up out of the canyon for a better view (Nathan and Noah did this while I stayed in the cabin packing things up with the other two)

After all that, we headed home. We left with plenty of dust to be washed off and a satisfaction remembered... of time with nature and each other. We arrived home thankful for the reintroduction to this long lost friend and with a renewed determination to make camping more a part of our family life.

{ REINTRODUCTION }
by Amanda Probst

Pick and choose.
While not a technical vacation (it was only overnight and within an hour of our house), this camping excursion was a great reintroduction to bigger family outings. Rather than ramble on about everything that happened, I selected a few highlights both for the photos and the journaling points. Quick, bite-size pieces to portray the whole.

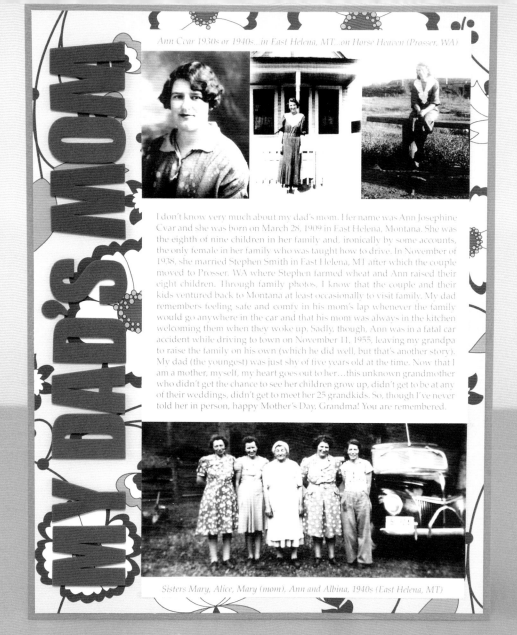

Ann Cvar 1930s or 1940s...in East Helena, MT...on Horse Heaven (Prosser, WA)

I don't know very much about my dad's mom. Her name was Ann Josephine Cvar and she was born on March 28, 1909 in East Helena, Montana. She was the eighth of nine children in her family and, ironically by some accounts, the only female in her family who was taught how to drive. In November of 1938, she married Stephen Smith in East Helena, MT after which the couple moved to Prosser, WA where Stephen farmed wheat and Ann raised their eight children. Through family photos, I know that the couple and their kids ventured back to Montana at least occasionally to visit family. My dad remembers feeling safe and comfy in his mom's lap whenever the family would go anywhere in the car and that his mom was always in the kitchen welcoming them when they woke up. Sadly, though, Ann was in a fatal car accident while driving to town on November 11, 1955, leaving my grandpa to raise the family on his own (which he did well, but that's another story). My dad (the youngest) was just shy of five years old at the time. Now that I am a mother, myself, my heart goes out to her...this unknown grandmother who didn't get the chance to see her children grow up, didn't get to be at any of their weddings, didn't get to meet her 25 grandkids. So, though I've never told her in person, happy Mother's Day, Grandma! You are remembered.

Sisters Mary, Alice, Mary (mom), Ann and Albina, 1940s (East Helena, MT)

{ MY DAD'S MOM }
by Amanda Probst

Tell what you know.

When it comes to scrapbooking an older photo it can be difficult to know what to journal about—especially if the subject of the photo is no longer with you. Here, I opted to simply list what I know about my grandma. I wish I knew more, but at least I've documented what I do know so my boys will know it too.

August always makes me think of vacations…trying to squeeze a last adventure or two into summer break. Even though I haven't been in school in five years now and even though we didn't go on a lot of vacations growing up, the association is still there. It just feels like the time of year to get out there and do something. With three young boys, we haven't done a whole heap of vacationing yet. Infants may travel well (or so some have told us), but toddlers are definitely a challenge. But, though part of me hates to admit it, the end of toddler-ville in this household is just around the corner. We're mostly looking forward to it. And we have a list. A list of places we'd like to visit.

Some are places we've never been to…

THE STATUTE OF LIBERTY
the Great Wall of china
the pyramids…

Some are places Nathan and I have been to that we'd like to see again…

the Grand Canyon
Biltmore Estate
THE TOWER OF LONDON…

Some are places one of us has been to that the others haven't…

FLORENCE, ITALY
the Eiffel Tower
Washington, D.C.…

Some are places that are unlikely…

the North Pole
the top of Mt. Everest
the moon…

This isn't even close to all of it. Our list is long (and we're constantly adding to it), but it's ours. And one of these days…soon…we're going to start tackling it.

our LIST

{ OUR LIST }
by Amanda Probst

Daydream about vacation destinations.

Short on actual vacation photos? When I wrote the journaling for this page, we didn't have any recent vacation photos—just a list of places we'd like to visit. Rather than miss out on vacation pages altogether, I created this one that focuses instead on where we'd like to travel.

FROM thE ♥

For teacher appreciation week we planned something extra special for your kindergarten teacher and her assistant. I purchased terra cotta pots from a local craft store and gave you access to my entire paint collection. You went to town painting the pots with your own special flair. Then we went to a local nursery where you picked out marigolds which you planted all on your own in your custom designed pots. This project was 100% all you from the painting to the flowers to the planting. We may have spent more time than if we had just bought your teachers flowers from the store but it was well worth it. A gift from the heart means so much more than anything money can buy.

may

{ FROM THE HEART }
by Summer Fullerton

Report an act of kindness.

Summer photographed her daughter making these wonderful potted flowers for her teachers. When your child does something to show appreciation, why not document it to let her know just how proud you are?

As a family of seven, we didn't do much traveling while I was growing up. When we did take trips, it was generally to visit relatives in Spokane or Seattle. That was back in the days before seat belts and car seats and portable dvds. We'd all pile into whatever vehicle we were driving at the time (my memories always feature the Suburban). Usually there would be some argument about the seating arrangements. For some reason the very back seats were the most coveted. Fortunately for me, preferential treatment came with age and I was the oldest. During the 3 to 4 hour trip, we could lie down or move around the car. There was usually a cooler somewhere with drinks and food. To pass the time, sometimes my mom would sing and often we'd play the alphabet game (where you have to find the letters of the alphabet in order on any signs you see while driving). My dad would be driving and we'd shout out to remind him to watch the road, as he tended to get distracted and veer while looking off toward the wheat fields at the side of the road. Our luggage was generally strapped to the top of the car (a process that took some doing on my dad's part before we departed). If we were lucky, we'd get to stop once for a bathroom break and possibly to get something to eat. I recognize now that a good part of the "point" was simply the time being together, even if it meant being confined in a car for hours. With all our various activities, it wasn't unusual for us all to have something different going on each day during the summer. So, they may not have been the "cool" vacations others took during summer vacation, but they meant an opportunity for us all to reconnect.

WISH YOU
ONTHE RD
WERE HERE

.....are we there yet?

IN THE CAR
by Amanda Probst

Reminisce about road trips.

I didn't have any specific road trips in mind when I created this page, but I knew I wanted to record my thoughts about our family vacations in general. Rather than talk about the destinations, I journaled about the journeys: the seating arrangements, bathroom breaks, car entertainment and so forth.

Play with your supplies.

Scrapbook supplies are for more than layouts. Here, Tiffany took some chipboard, patterned papers and photos and created a wonderful memory game for her daughter. Using photos of family members near and far, you can make a lovely game that also serves to remind your kids of relatives they might not see all the time.

2 — well check appt for Micah @ 2:30 south office

three 4 5 6 7 — Nancy's bday 8

9 10 — swim lessons → 11 12 13 — Nathan's birthday four teen — space class @ Discovery Science Center @ 10:30 am 15

16 17 — NCHA mtg @ 7pm 18 19 — National Aviation Day — Date night! 20 21 — co-op @ 10:00 am 22

23 — home from camping? 24 twenty five 26 — Women's Equality Day 27 28 29 — Back to Homeschool BBQ @ 4:30 pm

30 31

- Don't forget to RSVP for BBQ
- Make something for neighborhood potluck
- Get sleeping bags cleaned

{ AUGUST }
by Amanda Probst

Take to the road.

Or at least use license plates. Here I used number masks and stickers (as masks) and just had great fun with paint. I added the fun license-plate stickers to bring in the feeling of good old-fashioned road trips.

Monthly Info:
Birthstones: Jade, Peridot
Flower: Gladiolus
Astrological signs: Leo (July 23–Aug. 22),
Virgo (Aug. 23–Sept. 22)

MAY **journaling** and **photography** PROMPTS

DATE	JOURNALING JUMPSTARTS	PHOTO OPS
May 1: May Day	Do you have any May Day traditions?	May Day baskets full of flowers and candy May Day celebrations in your community
May 5: Cinco de Mayo	How do you celebrate your own heritage?	A local Cinco de Mayo celebration A family gathering
Second Sunday in May: Mother's Day	If you have kids, write about the best parts of motherhood. If you don't have kids, interview your mom.	Your mom Your grandma Your female friends who are moms
First Saturday in May: National Scrapbook Day	What do you love best about scrapbooking?	You and your friends scrapbooking together Your scrapbook supplies
First Week of May: National Teacher's Week	Write about the teachers in your life who influenced you the most.	Your children's teachers Your children's school School supplies
Last Monday in May: Memorial Day	How do you celebrate Memorial Day?	Family celebrations (like a barbecue or picnic) Family tombstones at the cemeteries you visit

AUGUST

VACATION. August is perfect for traveling—whether it's to faraway places or simply around your hometown. Be open to a change of scenery. Think about the places you see every day, those you'd like to see someday and those you plan to see soon. What do you need to do to get to those places? What will you pack?

"LIFE MOVES **PRETTY** FAST; IF YOU DON'T STOP AND **LOOK** AROUND **ONCE** IN A WHILE, YOU COULD **MISS** IT."
—*Ferris Bueller*

{JUNE}

some days, she added, i think about going too.

aunt grace's birthday

1

7

8

2

JUNE

SUMMER. Ah, summer. June is about that. Think Father's Day, last day of school, graduations and free time. In grade school, I remember tee ball games and lazy nights. In high school, I remember end-of-school-year water fights. In college, I remember those nervous first days at a new summer job. Though your perspective on summer may change over time, some things are constant. Throughout it all, for instance, I have always associated June with the cherry harvest. What does summer mean to you?

"PERSONALITY CAN OPEN DOORS . . . BUT ONLY **CHARACTER** CAN **KEEP** THEM OPEN."
—Elmer G. Letterman

JULY **journaling** and **photography** PROMPTS

DATE	JOURNALING JUMPSTARTS	PHOTO OPS
July 1 or 2: Canada Day	Interview your Canadian friends about what this holiday means to them.	The Canadian flag Maple leaves
July 2: World UFO Day	I don't know that this is a "real" holiday, but it's kind of fun. If you made up your own holiday, what would it be?	Space craft The science fiction fans in your life
July 4: Independence Day	How do you celebrate the Fourth of July?	Fireworks The expressions on your family member's faces as they watch fireworks
July 14: Bastille Day (French National Holiday)	How has your life been influenced by French culture?	The French flag Fashion or food Symbols of French culture
Last Sunday of July: Parents' Day	How did your parents (as a unit) affect your life?	Your parents Your step-parents You as a parent
July: Family Reunions	How does your family stay connected?	Family members, as individuals and groups Family reunion settings

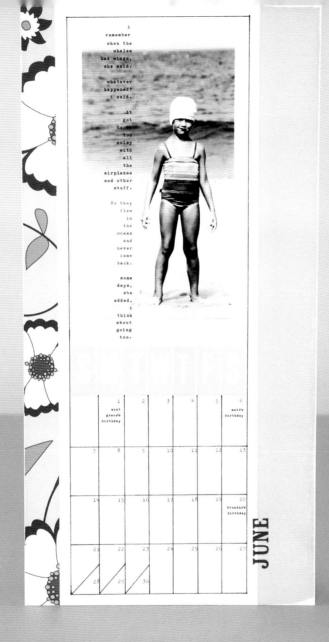

i remember when the whales had wings, she said.

whatever happened? i said.

it got to be too noisy with all the airplanes and other stuff.

So they flew in the ocean and never came back.

some days, she added, i think about going too.

	1 aunt grace's birthday	2	3	4	5	6 matt's birthday
7	8	9	10	11	12	13
14	15	16	17	18	19	20 brendan's birthday
21	22	23	24	25	26	27
28	29	30				

JUNE

{ JUNE }
by Laura Kurz

Go vertical.

I love how Laura made this calendar page in a 6" x 12" format! The extra space to the left of a younger Laura was perfect for a funny little quote about summer.

Monthly Info:
Birthstone: Pearl
Flower: Rose
Astrological signs: Gemini (May 21–June 20), Cancer (June 21–July 22)

We must not allow the clock & the calendar to blind us to the fact that each moment of life is a miracle & mystery.

- H. G. Wells

now

"NOW" CLOCK
by Amanda Probst

Forget the numbers.

It's summertime. Forget about hours and minutes and live in the moment. Enjoy the freedom of being without a watch. Live for now.

CHERRY HARVEST

June

For many people, the end of the school year meant summer vacation…lazy days by a pool or in a hammock, hanging out with friends, sleeping in. Starting in high school, summer vacation (at least the first part of it) for me meant cherry harvest. I remember the mornings, so brisk and just darn early (we're talking 4 am-ish). But, I loved seeing the sun rise shortly after my dad and I would arrive at the orchard for the day. Having discovered in short order that I wasn't cut out for actually picking the cherries (I was incredibly slow compared to "regular" pickers), I was in charge of checking each picker's boxes and tallying the count, basically keeping the records (something I was much better suited to). I walked beside the tractor all day as we made the circuit picking up every box, dumping them into bins by type and loading them to the pallets to be picked up later by truck. By the afternoons, I was always dusty, grimy and hot…usually more than ready for the work day to end. The day's challenges were welcome, though, on many counts. First, it meant I got to spend the day with my dad. I was able to really see him in action and learn more about what he does. Second, I was earning significant money (beyond just babysitting funds) for the first time, which was a gratifying experience. Third, and this may sound crazy, it was fun. The crew I worked with was often comprised of cousins and friends and we settled into an easy pattern to enjoy the day and each other's company. And fourth, being the traditionalist that I am, I truly enjoyed the sense of continuity from working on the family farm and being part of that cycle.

{ CHERRY HARVEST }
by Amanda Probst

Talk about a summer job.

Just looking at these photos makes me feel hot and grimy. But they also bring a deep feeling of satisfaction. I actually enjoyed working cherry harvest and am glad to have this layout to remember that.

Embrace history.

Living in Virginia provides Tiffany and her family the opportunity to visit numerous historical sites. During the summer of 2007, they commemorated America's 400th birthday by visiting the location of the pilgrims' first landing in 1607. Wish I could have joined them!

water

Since we homeschool, my boys don't really yet grasp the idea of summer vacation. Our daily routine does differ, though, during the summer. Mainly, the difference is the water. Summer for us means lots of water play...with sprinklers and water balloons and water guns and, when we can, pool time. The grins on Noah and Asher's faces when engaged in water revelry is priceless (as is the apprehension currently on Micah's, though I'm sure that will change with time). Ah. Summer.

{ JUST ADD WATER }

by Amanda Probst

Stop and think.

To make these fun "watery" letters, I simply dabbed some alcohol inks on acetate letters. I added a few drops of rubbing alcohol to dilute the inks and basically just played until I achieved the look I wanted.

Instead of heading to the park for typical Fourth of July booths and festivities this year, we did a little time travel. Yup, after a morning of Nathan taking the boys to see a radio controlled airplane show while I got some work done, we all headed to the local municipal airport to see World War II planes on display. Provisioned with plenty of water and sunscreen and a stroller for Micah, the boys delighted in seeing all of the planes out for show. Nathan lifted Noah and Asher so they could see inside cockpits and Noah took some pictures of his own. Next we got in line to do a walk-through tour of a B-17 bomber. It was a long line. Fortunately, the boys did a wonderful job of behaving themselves, venturing off with one of us every now and again to look at some of the old cars and motorcycles also on display or to see something on the WWII planes closer up. (There were also plenty of questions about WWII in general and ponderings as to why cars didn't used to have seat belts.) When we finally made it to the front of the line, Nathan, Noah and Asher climbed up and ventured through the B-17 while Micah and I waited. Once through, we opted not to get in the equally long line for the B-24 bomber also open to the public, instead heading home to rest a bit before the evening's fireworks.

"Mostly it's just amazing to me what they had back then and what they came up with." Noah, age 6.5

B★17

"I just liked getting to go through it, except for the bar thing (catwalk)...that was a little scary, but also fun." Asher, age 5

{ B-17 }
by Amanda Probst

Teach a history lesson.
We visited old World War II planes last Independence Day. We had all sorts of questions about how things worked and why they were needed. (Fortunately, my husband knew most of the answers.) In addition to being a wonderful opportunity to teach our sons about the history of our country, the old planes were just beautiful to photograph.

We celebrated Father's Day a weekend early this year with some quality family time. Though unsure whether taking Micah would work, we decided to give miniature golfing a go. The boys each eagerly grabbed a club and ball and we set off...with Micah in the backpack carrier to start. Little by little, the boys' technique is improving and their patience for the game went fairly well. We finally let Micah down around hole #11 and he surprised us by being very good, not chasing after his brothers' balls at all. He was obviously paying attention to all the golfing during the first part of the day, because he seemed to know just what to do. He was so adorably excited and let Nathan help him with his swing before impatiently dashing off to find the hole. I don't remember playing much miniature golf growing up and didn't even know the rules of golf until I got married. I can see, though, that this seems to be a right of passage. Nathan talks fondly of playing golf with his grandpa and dad, and I can clearly envision these boys doing the same one day. As far as fatherly traditions, I think this is a good one.

fathers & sons

{ FATHERS & SONS }

by Amanda Probst

Think about past generations.
This isn't only a layout about what we did to celebrate Father's Day. It's also about the relationship between fathers and sons in my husband's family through the generations. It's about golfing together and how we hope to continue this tradition with our own sons.

leaving your mark

my hero ★

proud of you

This was a beautiful day. Exactly five years from the day you became a Captain, you were promoted to Major. However, this was unlike any ceremony I had ever seen. You chose to have your promotion ceremony in the Casemate Museum at Fort Monroe, standing in front of a Civil War flag. One room away from where Jefferson Davis' prison cell. The same building where Edgar Allan Poe once resided and where so many slaves found refuge during the war. History surrounded us the entire day, and this was the place that you chose.

I know that I do not tell you enough just how proud of you I am. Yes, I complain about the many moves that we have endured throughout your career and the countless hours that I spent alone while you fought for our country half a world away. Yet, through it all, you became more of a hero to me than you were the day before. We thank you for giving us a part of the liberty our family enjoys every day. Our children know that the uniform you wear is something special and you are special in it.

You do not have much time left as an officer in the Army; when January 2008 commences, your 10 ½ years of service will be complete. Your plans to leave it are for us, so that we may enjoy more stability in our lives. I know that is a painful decision for you to make, but I appreciate it. I will never forget just how much of a difference you have made while you wore this uniform, and my pride in you will never, ever wane. I love you.

Casemate Museum, Dec. 1, 2007

{ I'M PROUD OF YOU }
by Tracey Odachowski

Celebrate freedom.

For his final promotion ceremony as an officer in the army, Tracey's husband chose to have the ceremony in an old Civil War fort. What an awesome way to blend past and present! Do you have access to any historical sites?

a taste of
SUMMER

When I was little I remember having butterflies in my tummy the night before my parents would take us to Busch Gardens. Twenty years later, I finally had the privilege to take you! They didn't have Land of the Dragons when I was a kid but I had read up on their new attractions and whipped out your new bathing suit as soon as we saw the first dragon. The smile on your face was priceless. You were a little apprehensive at first to jump right in the water-play park but eventually you caught on and spent the entire morning dodging high-powered water streams and other little youngsters. You definitely felt the cool splash which made it all the more fun.

You cried when we left but I know we'll be back. We've got season summer passes!

{ A TASTE OF SUMMER }
by Tiffany Tillman

Introduce a tradition.

What fun! Tiffany introduced her daughter to the thrills of Busch Gardens, something she enjoyed herself as a child. With summer passes, she's sure to instill a similar love in her daughter. A summer tradition is born!

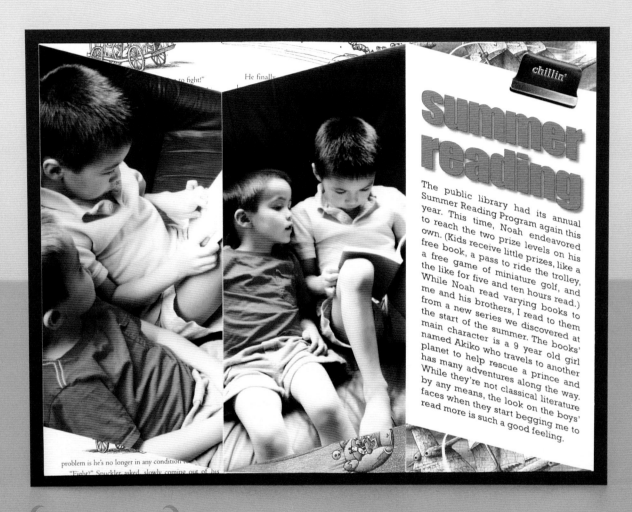

chillin'

summer reading

The public library had its annual Summer Reading Program again this year. This time, Noah endeavored to reach the two prize levels on his own. (Kids receive little prizes, like a free book, a pass to ride the trolley, a free game of miniature golf, and the like for five and ten hours read.) While Noah read varying books to me and his brothers, I read to them from a new series we discovered at the start of the summer. The books' main character is a 9 year old girl named Akiko who travels to another planet to help rescue a prince and has many adventures along the way. While they're not classical literature by any means, the look on the boys' faces when they start begging me to read more is such a good feeling.

{ SUMMER READING }
by Amanda Probst

Read a book.
This summer, remember to document what you (and your kids) read. It's a great glimpse into what you were interested in at the time. Plus, reading is a wonderful outlet for the imagination. With a good book, you're free to be anything!

Look at you. My precious baby. My third son. Would you please stop growing up? Pretty please? I just adore this baby stage...this chubby cheeked, easily amused, not able to talk back, cuddly little baby stage. Okay, I suppose that if I were honest with myself I adore all the stages. I love the fresh newborn smell, the first belly laugh, the discovery of the feet... And I know that I'll love what's to come just as much...the curiosity of the toddler, the development of your true personality, the ability to converse with you in full sentences and be amazed by how your brain works. Yet I can't help wanting to simply pause life every now and again and keep you just as you are; perhaps even rewind and just re-live some of your earlier wonderfulness. Maybe it's because you're my third and probably last baby. Maybe you actually are cuter than your brothers (hee hee). Maybe I'm getting old. I don't really care what it is. I just know that I want to remember this moment always...you...sitting on a blanket at the park...watching your brothers launch air rockets while discovering the joys of grass...putting up with us though you really just wanted to take a nap. You're so, incredibly, sweet. Tomorrow you'll be different. Sweeter? Probably. But that doesn't take away from the beauty of today. So, when you're all grown up with children of your own and I'm still longing for this precious baby and simultaneously looking forward to seeing what more you'll become, please remember every now and again to simply pause and appreciate it all. Trust me.

handsome playful rugged fun
cute gentleman handsome
playful rugged fun cute
gentleman handsome playful
rugged fun cute gentleman

PAUSE

PAUSE
by Amanda Probst

Slow down.

I love this picture. If you're a mother, you know how I wish I could stop time or at least slow it down a little. Thanks to scrapbooking, though, I can preserve moments like this. Taken on Father's Day 2006, this photo and the accompanying journaling fit in so nicely with summertime—a time for slowing down and living life at a more leisurely pace.

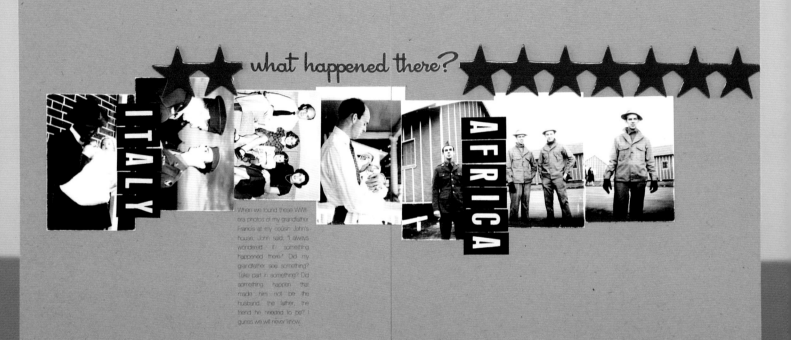

The layout photos contain the words: **what happened there?**, **ITALY**, and **AFRICA**.

The journaling text reads: When we found these WWII-era photos of my grandfather Francis at my cousin John's house, John said, "I always wondered if something happened there." Did my grandfather see something? Take part in something? Did something happen that made him not be the husband, the father, the friend he needed to be? I guess we will never know.

{ WHAT HAPPENED? }

by Laura Kurz

Leave questions unanswered.

Sometimes you just won't know what was happening in an old photo. Rather than hide it away, scrapbook it and simply voice your questions. Better to have it displayed so you can wonder and guess than have it tucked away in a box.

summer is

feasting on watermelon for breakfast, lunch and dinner ... fresh flowers from the farmers market ... running through the fountain at Tualatin Commons at 8 o'clock at night ... hearing the ice cream truck 5 blocks away and convincing your sister to buy you a popsicle ... cruising around the neighborhood on your scooter ... lathering up with sun screen ... and many back yard water fights all in the name of staying cool ...

{ SUMMER IS . . . }
by Summer Fullerton

Make your own definition.

Journaling doesn't have to be difficult. Simply list everything that comes to mind when you think of summer. Easy. By the way, I love how Summer matted the photos to look like Polaroid shots and added detail to the title with stamps and embossing powder. Fun!

{ BLISS }
by Amanda Probst

Blow bubbles.

Bubbles. Who can resist? I guarantee that if you get a bubble machine and a toddler together, you will get awesome photos. Look at my cutie, so uninhibited and free! Also, note how I cut the cardstock and placed a transparency behind it to create "bubbles" of my own.

What Daddy does:

(according to Noah & Asher)…
plays with us, makes the money, works, builds model rockets with us,
gives us baths, takes out the garbage, mows the grass, gives Micah food,
takes us out on special nights, takes us grocery shopping, makes dinner and last calls,
plays games with us, reads to us, talks on his phone, uses his computer,
plays golf on his phone with us, helps Mommy sometimes, rough-houses with us…

loves us.

{ WHAT DADDY DOES }
by Amanda Probst

Ask for a different perspective.

When I set out to scrapbook these photos of my husband, I planned to journal about how proud I am of him. Somehow, the focus of my layout changed: I decided to ask the boys what they thought their daddy does at work. I love their responses and think the layout is even more touching with the journaling in their own words.

We lived in the country and I don't remember ever going into town to see the fireworks displays on the Fourth of July. I'm sure they had them. We just didn't ever go. Instead, we would trek to one of the temporary tents selling fireworks and buy whatever my dad and brothers generally agreed upon (not usually too much, just enough to have a little fun). (As my brothers got older, I remember them saving their own money to add to the purchase. Personally, I didn't see the point in spending my money on something we were just going to light on fire.)

We were allowed to set off a few of the smaller fireworks on the patio near the house (things like those little snakes that grow when you light one end and pop its and very small things). For the bigger stuff, we'd clear a spot in the driveway/gravel behind the house and light them off after dark…creating our own little fireworks show. I left the act of lighting everything to my dad and brothers (never have cared for matches or lighting things) and definitely remember a time or two that they didn't get away from things quick enough and wound up breathing smoke like a dragon.

Nowadays, I find that I enjoy the large city fireworks displays and we take the boys to see them, finding a grassy spot in the park to sit and watch with everyone else. Personally, I much prefer the big overhead explosions to little ones right at hand…bigger show, no money out of pocket, no danger of sparks, less to clean up. I love watching the fascination on their little faces and hearing them "ooh" and "ahh." I know, though, that as they get older they'll want to buy some of the personal fireworks. I suppose that will be okay…so long as no one expects me to do any of the lighting. In the meantime, I'll just enjoy the big shows and watching their delight.

{ FIREWORKS }
by Amanda Probst

Capture the expression as well as the explosion.

I probably annoyed the heck out of the people sitting near us during this fireworks display. I couldn't help it: I had to use the flash at least a few times so I could photograph the boys' reactions as well as the fireworks themselves!

Summer Foods

Canteloupe Steamed blue crabs corn on the cob Watermelon

Strawberries Squash my birthday cake! Shrimp & Old Bay

Sure to make my mouth water.

{ MY FAVORITE
SUMMER FOODS }
by Tracey Odachowski

Think with your stomach.
What summer scrapbook would be complete without detailing your favorite summer foods? I love the close-ups here; it's almost like Tracey was making her own personal menu!

Growing up, summers were busy times for our family. My dad had his hands full with cherry harvest much of June and then wheat harvest in July and August before gearing up for apple harvest in September. Evenings were often occupied with coaching a mini ball team for one or more of my brothers and sisters or attending my sister's swim meets. Somehow, though, the Fourth of July often found us with a few days respite. Some years, we would take advantage of those breaks and head to East Helena, Montana…where we would visit with my dad's Aunt Beana (his mom's youngest sister) and Uncle Elmer. They had a cabin up in the nearby mountains that we loved to visit. My dad would try his hand at fishing in the little creek that ran right next to the cabin, and we'd even hike up to the Continental Divide. Sometimes other relatives would join us there for a full family gathering. Sometimes not. Either way, we'd also head back into town for the fireworks displays over the smelting yards and be sure to visit Smith's Place just down the road from my great aunt and uncle's house. Then we'd pile back in the car for the long ride home…back to our regularly scheduled busyness.

{ MONTANA IN JULY }
by Amanda Probst

Remember a place.

Where did you spend the Fourth of July when you were growing up? I spent most of mine at home, but we celebrated at least a handful in Montana. Those are the ones I remember most.

"WHAT 2 DO" JAR
by Amanda Probst

Spin for inspiration.

At a loss for what to do with your kids this summer? Make this handy little activity jar! I sat down with my boys one day and listed all sorts of ideas, then broke them into categories. We put the ideas in this jar (color-coded by category) and made a spinner—and now we have a quick solution for the "what to do blues." This would also work great when you need inspiration in other areas of your life . . . like techniques to try on your layouts or movies to rent when you're feeling indecisive!

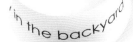

JULY

sunday	monday	tuesday	wednesday	thursday	friday	saturday
			1 Canada Day	**2**	**3**	**4** Independence day
5 bbq @ julies	**6**	**7**	**8**	**9**	**10**	**11**
12	**13**	**14**	**15**	**16** 162 days til christmas	**17**	**18** mge co. picnic
19	**20**	**21** dentist apt 2 pm	**22**	**23**	**24**	**25**
26 parents day	**27**	**28**	**29**	**30**	**31**	

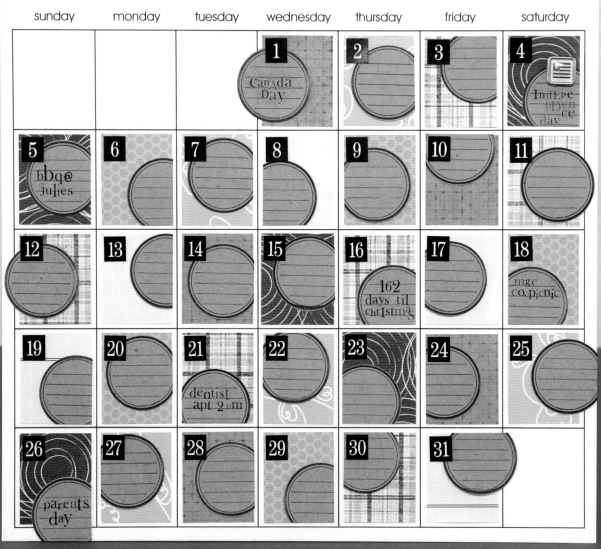

{ JULY }
by Summer Fullerton

Use a journaling stamp.

I love how Summer made use of a journaling spot stamp for this calendar page! The random pattern of both the colored papers and the journaling circles gives this page such a feeling of joy and freedom.

Monthly Info:
Birthstone: Ruby
Flowers: Larkspur, Water Lily
Astrological signs: Cancer (June 21–July 22), Leo (July 23–Aug. 22)

JUNE **journaling** and **photography** PROMPTS

DATE	JOURNALING JUMPSTARTS	PHOTO OPS
June 14: Flag Day	If you designed your own family flag, what would you include on it and why?	Flags Patriotic symbols
Third Sunday in June: Father's Day	Write about something amazing you learned from your father.	Your dad Your grandpa Your male friends who are dads
June 20: First Day of Summer	What do you like best about summer?	Sunglasses Swimming suits Beach toys
Third Saturday of June: National Hollerin' Day	This North Carolina holiday celebrates the art of "hollerin'" as a way to communicate over distances without a phone. How would you communicate if there were no phones?	A cell phone Communication devices, like a Blackberry or your instant-messenger program
End of June: Last Day of School	How do you feel when school's out for the summer?	Your children arriving home on the last day of school Classroom parties
End of June: Graduation	Write about a graduation ceremony that impacted your life.	Diplomas Tassels Graduates in their robes Graduation parties

JULY

FREEDOM. From backyard barbecues to fireworks displays, July is about celebrating freedom. Freedom, though, has more than one definition. On Independence Day, we in the United States celebrate our liberty. But freedom can also simply mean the absence of obligations. Consider both perspectives and the roles they play in your life this summer. After all, July is the halfway mark of the year . . . a good time to stop and evaluate.

"HOW **BEAUTIFUL** IT IS **TO** DO NOTHING AND THEN **REST** AFTERWARD!"
—*Spanish Proverb*

MONTH *by* MONTH
SCRAPBOOKING
by Amanda Probst

JULY–DECEMBER
(FLIP BOOK)